Praise for Tom Stone

"Tom Stone has done something quite unique. He has distilled out of his vast experience the simplest and most useful tools for creating profound and lasting change in our lives. I am truly grateful to Tom for his help in my own life and I am delighted that he is sharing his insights and techniques to help others on a large scale. I know his desire is very similar to mine—to have a positive impact on the lives of many, many people. I know that through his pioneering work in Human Software Engineering he will accomplish this goal in a profound and powerful way."

—Jack Canfield, Co-author, *Chicken Soup for the Soul®* series and *The Success Principles™: How to Get from Where You Are to Where You Want to Be.*

"Tom Stone is nothing short of a genius. He is an expert in the area of dynamics, and he has the cleanest energy of ANYONE I've ever met, bar none. Even good coaches make an average of 20 coaching mistakes per session, but when I met with Tom, he made only one mistake—and then he immediately caught himself and corrected it! I was really amazed, and I immediately asked him to be my personal coach. I guess that makes him the coach to the coach to the coaches!"

—Thomas Leonard, Founder of *CoachVille* and Life Coaching Industry Pioneer

Praise for *Pure Awareness*

"The Pure Awareness Techniques that Tom Stone shares in this book have had a profound effect on my life. I became involved in the field of energy psychology early on and I believe that these methods can be used by every therapist, counselor, addiction specialist, life coach, and anyone who is interested in improving their life. I think you will be amazed and delighted at how rapid and simple these transformational tools are to practice."

—George J. Pratt, Ph.D., Chairman, Psychology, Scripps Memorial Hospital, La Jolla, Coauthor, *Instant Emotional Healing: Acupressure for the Emotions*

"I've used these techniques on a daily basis and continue to do so. As a result, today I experience a sense of continuous inner peace and connection with my Self."

—Colleen Moore, Licensed Marriage and Family Therapist, Auburn, CA

Praise for *Core Dynamics Coaching*

"After attending the Core Dynamics training in Phoenix, I threw away every other coaching strategy and tool I've ever learned because I don't need them anymore. People are coming from all over for appointments and are reporting transformations of mind-blowing proportions. There is no way to overstate the importance of the Core Dynamics training for coaching."

—Wendy Down, Master Certified Coach

"We may have come to some wrong conclusions in the past and the Core Dynamics method showed me how I could update my perspective to be more successful and effective both in business and in life. We often think that logic and intellect should be the only driver for business, but in the Core Dynamics Coach Training, I was shown how much power is available to us when we use all of who we are, including our emotions."

—Val Williams, Master Certified Coach

About the Author

Tom Stone is an internationally acclaimed coach and speaker, and an accomplished inventor, entrepreneur and writer. He has spent much of his life developing the most efficient and effective techniques for solving problems using principles and techniques from biophysics.

Tom is the pioneer of the new emerging field of Human Software Engineering (HSE) in which he has made a number of unique discoveries, including a set of profound insights into the nature of human conditioning, called the CORE DYNAMICS OF COMMON PROBLEMS. This unique body of work provides the tools for easily eliminating the barriers and blocks that keep people from having the life they truly want.

Tom has turned his focus in recent years to finding effective solutions to many of the seemingly intractable problems that plague modern society, such as anxiety, depression and ADD/ADHD. This book is the culmination of several years of intensive research and is the first in the *Vaporize Your Problems* series. Tom lives in Carlsbad, California with his wife Lynda, where he directs the Great Life Coaching Institute.

To learn more about Tom's work, please visit

www.vaporizeyouranxiety.com

The *Vaporize Your Problems* Book Series
Little Books with Big Solutions

VAPORIZE YOUR ANXIETY

Without Drugs or Therapy

TOM STONE

Vaporize Your Anxiety

without Drugs or Therapy

Published by:
Great Life Technologies, LLC
7040 Avenida Encinas, Suite 104 #380
Carlsbad, CA 92011
(619) 557-2700
www.greatlifetechnologies.com

978-1605859002

This book is dedicated to everyone who would like to be free from anxiety.

Acknowledgments

I am most grateful to my wife Lynda who has always supported me wholeheartedly in my work and creative projects like the writing of this and my other books.

I would also especially like to thank my editors David Jacoby and Aimee Snow for their great job of transforming my manuscript into a polished book. And an additional thanks to Aimee for the superb job with the graphics and graphics revisions for the book. I would also like to thank Cathi Stevenson for her beautiful cover design.

I am deeply grateful to Michael Stratford for his contribution to the special application of the GAP technique called SANYAMA and his delightful collaboration in co-creating and teaching the Core Dynamics Coach Training Program with me.

I am particularly grateful to all of my clients, seminar and training program participants, the Core Dynamics Coaches and Teachers, the WaveMaker Coaches and Human Software Engineers who have so wholeheartedly embraced this work and who have provided an environment in which these techniques could be refined and perfected over the years. It is these pioneers of Human Software Engineering who are really propagating this work in the world. To all of you I offer my heartfelt thanks.

And I am grateful to you, dear reader, for having the courage to open these pages and explore new solutions to the age-old problem of anxiety. May you use and enjoy the precious techniques presented here and may they help you to Vaporize Your Anxiety for the rest of your life!

Tom Stone
Carlsbad, California
February 2008

Disclaimer

The information both in this book and published elsewhere by Great Life Technologies is not intended to replace the services of a physician or psychiatric care. Our approach is not for everyone, and is in no way meant to diagnose, treat, or cure any disease or psychiatric disorder. You should consult a physician in all matters relating to your health, particularly in respect to any symptoms that may require diagnosis or medical attention.

Contents

How to use this book

This book will provide you with tools and techniques you can start using *today* that will liberate you from the grip of anxiety, without the use of drugs or traditional therapy. My experience guiding many hundreds of people with these techniques has demonstrated that relief from anxiety and worry can occur within minutes of learning and using them. Although they are probably very different from anything you've experienced before, they are quite easy to learn. And as you'll see, once you begin practicing them, a whole new world will open up to you, allowing you to experience more joy, fulfillment, and success than you ever thought possible.

You see, when powerful emotional problems are literally vaporized, it becomes possible, perhaps for the first time in your life, to step away from your suffering. This is a profound experience because many of us are so completely identified with our suffering. When you're free of it, you become present for life's greatest gift: the true experience of who and what you really are. You'll suddenly find that you don't spend time *questioning* who you are any more, so much as *experiencing* who you are. You'll find that you have access to the one thing that makes true happiness and productivity possible. It's the thing we're all after, and it's the one thing that for many of us seems so out of reach: *Peace of Mind.*

Now, I understand that these are big promises, and I need to emphasize that just *reading* this book will not free you from worry and anxiety. You'll need to put the techniques into *practice* and you'll need to *remember to use them*. But when you do this, you'll find that you've gone beyond putting a band-aid on your anxiety. You will have actually *resolved* the problems at their core, so if anxiety rears its ugly head again you'll know just how to resolve it quickly and thoroughly. What I've found time after time is that anyone can be freed from anxiety when they use these tools consistently and diligently.

Part I of *Vaporize Your Anxiety* is a discussion of the various theories and research that form the foundation of the techniques we use. Those of you who have not had any familiarity with my work should be sure to read this section. I cover all the relevant information you'll need to understand how you're going to proceed.

Part II of the book is a practical guide, giving you exercises and instructions so you can begin to Vaporize Your Anxiety right away.

Note: Undoubtedly, some readers of this book will already be familiar with my work from my other books and from the many seminars I teach every year. These readers may wish to skip directly to Part II of the book, where I speak specifically about the techniques used for vaporizing your anxiety. However, since the material in Part I is the cornerstone of my approach, it would be beneficial to everyone, regardless of their experience, to read Part I in its entirety. This is particularly so because I have not, in my previous work, addressed the issue of anxiety in depth, as I have done here.

To Your Health and Well-being,
Tom

Vaporize Your Anxiety

without Drugs or Therapy

Part I
The Problem

chapter 1

Facing the Challenge of Anxiety

The Scope of the Problem

According to the Anxiety Disorders Association of America (ADAA), an estimated 40 million Americans over the age of 18 suffer from an anxiety disorder.[1] Anxiety disorders are therefore the most common mental illness in the U.S., with over 18% of the adult U.S. population affected. That means that one in seven adults in the U.S. are struggling with anxiety on an ongoing basis. Further, approximately one third of American adults will have at least one anxiety or panic attack in their lifetimes. This startling data reveals that anxiety is the most prevalent emotional disorder in the U.S.—more common even than alcohol abuse or depression.

According to "The Economic Burden of Anxiety Disorders," a study commissioned by the ADAA and based on data gathered by the association and published in the Journal of Clinical Psychiatry, anxiety disorders cost the U.S. more than $42 billion a year—almost one third of the $148 billion total mental health bill for the U.S. More than $22.8 billion of those costs are associated with the repeated use of healthcare services, as those with anxiety disorders seek relief for symptoms that mimic physical illnesses. Indeed, people with an anxiety disorder are three-to-five times more likely to go to the doctor and six times more likely to be hospitalized for psychiatric disorders than non-sufferers.[2]

1 http://www.adaa.org/AboutADAA/PressRoom/Stats&Facts.asp
2 ibid

These figures make it clear that we are in the midst of a mental health crisis. Worse, for all our supposed medical sophistication, we don't even seem to be making a dent in the problem. We self-medicate, we seek therapists, and yet we stay anxious. What can be done?

What *is* Anxiety, Really?

While there are many theories about anxiety and how to deal with it, I take a very simple approach based on practical, experiential wisdom. Although this book endeavors to offer penetrating and valuable insights into why humans tend to develop anxiety, my main interest is offering you techniques that will help to rapidly and thoroughly resolve this widespread problem.

This work looks beyond a strictly biochemical or genetic point of view and considers instead that the experience of anxiety occurs as the result of being stuck at the outer edges of fear—afraid, in a sense, of the deeper, overwhelming energy of fear—without proper tools or training to resolve it. When this happens, fear continues to be held in the body without resolution. Anxiety is simply our body's attempt to avoid being overwhelmed by fear; it keeps us from having to face the true epicenter of our emotion. This "coping strategy" (that is, trying to avoid being overwhelmed by the energy of the fear) is the best we can do, so we stay stuck in an eternal, anxious dance around the outer edges of fear.

The reason we reach this state is that we haven't learned to effectively resolve intense emotions and traumas. Our early childhood conditioning compounds the problem, and while not everyone experiences problems with anxiety, this underlying conditioning does appear to be pretty universal. And as you will see from reading Chapter 4 on the ACE Study, the severity of the conditioning can determine why some people have problems with anxiety and others don't.

Human Software Engineering

The insights and techniques taught in this book were developed as a part of an emerging field called Human Software Engineering™, which is based on the idea that humans are a lot like computers. After all, we created computers to automate certain human tasks, so it makes sense that in many ways, they behave like we do. And as computers become more sophisticated, they become more and more like us. What is interesting is that we can learn some very useful things about ourselves by thinking about how computers work. As it turns out, terms like "software," "hardware," "virus," and "bugs" all are surprisingly effective for describing both what's going on with us, and how to improve it.

It is true, of course, that computers are much less complicated than we are. In fact, any researcher in the field of neuroscience will tell you that the human brain is infinitely more complex than even the biggest most complex computer on earth. So our capacity to research, create and understand the most complex computers is by no means a substitute for the study of the brain (a field that's still in its infancy, really). But on a metaphorical level, thinking about computers can give us a great deal of insight into how we work.

Really, a computer is just a device that does two things: it receives requests and it responds to them. So for example, when you open up your email account and you hit "get new mail," you're just making a request to the computer, and the computer responds by putting all your new emails into your inbox. Obviously, it's a little more complicated than that, but in the simplest terms, "request then response" is all that's really ever happening in your computer, or even when you're using the Internet.

Now, when your computer is running an old version of an operating system or a particular software program, or if there's a bug in the system somewhere, communication breaks down. The flaw prevents the computer from responding correctly, or in some cases, from responding at all. For example, you might double click on a document to try to open it, but if you don't have the software program the document was created with, or if your old operating system can't support the program, your computer won't give you any response (except maybe "I can't give you a response," i.e., "Program Not Found").

If you do have the program, but there happens to be a bug somewhere in the document or in your software program, you might open it up and see a bunch of gobbledygook. Have you ever opened up a web page or a document and seen a bunch of squares and slashes and circles? Your computer is giving you a response—it's just the wrong one.

Much like computers, humans have "bugs" too. For some people, these bugs cause procrastination or anger, or even addictive behaviors. And for many others, they cause anxiety and anxiety-related emotional problems. Think about this for a moment: scroll through your daily life and stop to think about your "problems." If you're like most people, you probably have a handful of problems that keep coming up, over and over. Maybe it's having the nerve to speak your mind to superiors at work, or to your spouse. Maybe it's eating certain foods you know aren't good for you. Maybe it's something as simple as being lazy about flossing!

If you think about it, you will realize that in each case, what's happening is that you're making a request—"Could you please talk to your boss about how ridiculously low your salary is?"—but you're getting either no response ("Sorry, didn't hear you. I think I'll go get a cup of coffee and then go back to my desk"), or you're getting the wrong response entirely (you go talk to your boss, but when you open your mouth, what comes out is something like "I love your new suit! Oh, and by the way, I'm really enjoying that new project. Okay, see you later!" And you walk dejectedly back to your desk.)

Another metaphor that is very helpful in the context of Human Software Engineering is that of the old operating system that won't allow you to run newer, more sophisticated programs. You may have had the experience of getting some great new software for your computer, only to find out that you can't actually use it unless you upgrade your operating system. Much in the same way, you can spend lots of time learning new techniques and strategies and philosophies for improving your life in one way or another, but if you're still stuck inside all the old conditioning from your childhood (that is, your old operating system), none of those techniques will ever really work in the long term. You'll end up with a shelf full of books you've diligently read, and all the same problems you had when your bookshelf was empty.

The tools in this book, as well as the exclusive audio recordings we've made available for you at www.VaporizeYourAnxiety.com, will teach you how to literally "debug" your "inner human software," "upgrade" your "operating system," and in the process, quickly reduce and very likely eliminate your anxiety completely. As I said earlier, however, to have true success with these techniques, it is very important to learn them thoroughly and to remember to use them regularly. I can't stress this enough. Please read this book from start to finish, and take the time to stop and practice when indicated. Practice lots and lots. Once you start to get a feel for the techniques, you'll find yourself doing them almost effortlessly.

In this book, you're going to learn to do some things that are in many cases the exact opposite of what you've been deeply conditioned to do. But the truth is, they are really quite natural and anyone can easily learn to do them, even though they may seem strange and unfamiliar at first. And besides, if you have come to the realization that what you've been doing up until now hasn't gotten rid of your anxiety, it's safe to assume that something "really different" is *exactly* what you need.

There is one other thing I would like to mention here. If you've been experiencing anxiety for a long time, the idea that you can eliminate it quickly and completely might sound a bit unreal. In fact, it might be enough to trigger anxiety about whether or not this could possibly be true, because it sounds like such an outrageous claim. But so many people have been successful with vaporizing their anxiety using these techniques that I feel compelled to share these great breakthroughs with everyone who suffers unnecessarily from anxiety. I sincerely hope that you will apply these techniques consistently so that you too can vaporize your anxiety and be free to live as you wish.

At several points in the book, there will be exercises for you to practice. Because the techniques are experiential rather than intellectual, doing the exercises is very important. If you'd like to get some help with this, we have many highly trained coaches who can guide you through the process over the phone. In fact, it is a testament to the power of these techniques that many of these coaches began as clients of mine. They were so impressed with the results they achieved personally that they became coaches themselves, so they could help others overcome their obstacles in life. You can learn more about our coaches at **www.VaporizeYourAnxiety.com/coaches.html**

To further help you along the path to Vaporizing Your Anxiety, we have set up a wonderful resources area at the Vaporize Your Anxiety website. Here you'll find audio and video recordings as well as many links that will help you get the most out of the book. Just visit **www.VaporizeYourAnxiety.com/resources.html**

chapter 2
The Set Up

How Preverbal Conditioning Sets us Up to be Anxious

Before we get into the actual techniques, I would like to take a moment to explain how they came about. Human Software Engineering and the techniques for vaporizing your anxiety are based on a set of profound insights into the nature of what is called "pre-verbal human conditioning." These insights came over many years of research into what happens before we have words to describe our experiences.

As it turns out, anxiety, like many of the emotional problems that plague us in our adult lives, is the result of things we took on as decisions about life and about ourselves before we had words to describe them. When we're very young—one, two, three years old—we don't have language yet. But even though we don't have words, we do have something else in great abundance: FEELINGS! We may not have names for these feelings yet, but we *have* them and we live inside them every moment of every day.

At that young age, we are often confronted with situations that make us feel emotionally overwhelmed. Because there are so many of these situations we must face, and because the feeling of being emotionally overwhelmed is so uncomfortable, we end up making a *feeling-level decision—a pre-verbal decision*—to put a lid on accessing our own innate capacity to feel, in an attempt to mitigate the problem of getting overwhelmed emotionally. The problem is that in our early life, we make a whole lot of these decisions about life and about ourselves.

This conception of how pre-verbal conditioning operates has been borne out by extensive scientific research on emotions and the brain. Using the newest generation of brain scanning devices, researchers have discovered cells in the brain that are directly responsible for processing emotional experiences. While being scanned, subjects were given emotional stimuli, and the brain cells that were activated were monitored. These cells—called "spindle cells"—experienced increased blood flow during the period of emotional stimulation. These findings leave little doubt that spindle cells are involved with the processing of emotional information[3].

In addition, it was discovered that there are *relatively few spindle cells in our brain during infancy*. So when we're still very young, we really don't have much capacity to feel and process our emotions.

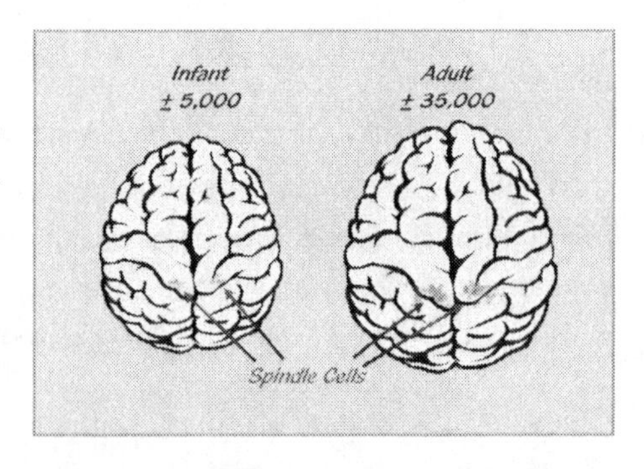

We just don't have the "physical hardware" to do it. But between infancy and adulthood, there is apparently about a sevenfold increase in the number of spindle cells in the brain, and therefore a substantial increase in our capacity to experience a wider range of emotions. What this means is that as we grow, our bodies and brains acquire more and more "hardware" for processing feelings. But because we've been conditioned to avoid intense emotional experiences, this increased capacity tends to be grossly underutilized. Our operating system is in desperate need of updating. The old myth that "humans only use ten percent of their brains" has generally been debunked, but when it comes to our ability to feel, it looks like this may actually be quite accurate!

3 Blakeslee, Sandra. "Humanity? Maybe It's in the Wiring." New York Times, December 9, 2003.

Underutillization of our Innate Capacity to Feel

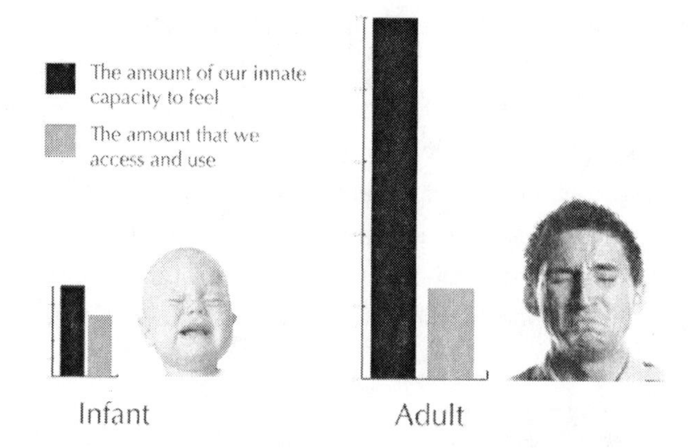

For example, one day during your first years, you might get an inspiration to do something. Say, give your sister a haircut, or finger-paint the dog. And what happens? Your parents find out, and you get punished. All of a sudden, your source of supply for everything—love, food, and protection—turns on you. And what is it that you got punished for? Essentially, it was for acting in a very pure way, based on an inner creative impulse. You didn't think. You just felt inspiration, and acted. So you make another of these feeling-level decisions. And this one is: "I'm not going to act on my creative intuition, because when I do, I get cut off from the things I need more than anything else in the whole world, and that's emotionally overwhelming." (Of course we don't think these words—it's just a feeling-level decision.)

So all these pre-verbal, feeling-level decisions keep us from experiencing our emotions fully. Because we get overwhelmed, and then punished, and then eventually decide to simply put a lid on our capacity to feel our feelings fully, we end up with a kind of storehouse of incomplete emotional experiences.

And then, right as we were building up a stockpile of these incomplete emotional experiences, something very curious happens. At about the age of three or four, we begin to make an enormous shift, and we start relating to the world primarily through words. Where once we were "pre-verbal," we are now "verbal." And as a result, we forget that we made all these feeling-level decisions in the first place. We forget the whole stockpile of incomplete emotional experiences and these also continue to accumulate. However, the incredible thing that my research into Human Software Engineering has shown is that even though we didn't have words, we were still capable of making very real, lasting decisions about ourselves and about the world around us.

When we "became verbal," however, we lost access to a real connection with the feeling-level world we lived in previously, and in which we made all those important, early decisions. We literally "crossed into the world of words," and lost our ability to change these decisions, because they were non-verbal, and they just don't respond to words. That's why anxiety—which is a direct result of these pre-verbal, feeling-level decisions—is typically so resistant to change using traditional therapy or self-help books. It's a little like trying to *see* music, or *touch* the scent of a cake baking. It's just the wrong set of tools.

So the problem we face as adults is that although we've forgotten them, these feeling-level decisions are still lodged in our consciousness at a very deep level, beyond what we can describe. And unfortunately, they tend to dictate everything we do. We live inside their incredibly limiting influence without even realizing it, cut off from the experience of who we really are. My research over the last 14 years has been focused primarily on discovering what the real bugs are that junk up our inner human software. What I've discovered is that for the most part, it's those same feeling-level decisions—the same pre-verbal conditioning. And it is this very kind of *preverbal, feeling-level decision* that is the *real* basis of anxiety. Anxiety itself is really nothing but the inability to fully experience the intense emotional energy of fear that is held in the body.

Of course, the question is, "What can we do about it?" To answer this, we need to talk a little bit about feelings, but in a different way than you may be used to.

Just what *are* feelings, anyway?

One of the foundational principles of quantum mechanics is that everything is produced out of a field of pure potentiality, a limitless field of pure energy and information that has not yet become expressed in any physical form. The theory is that everything we experience is created from this field of pure potential. And everything, say the quantum physicists, is energy: the book you're holding in your hands, the bones in your body, the windshield on your car. So if everything is energy, this must also include our feelings.

This is not really so hard to understand. In fact, we know instinctively that our brains and bodies create the experience of emotion as an energetic response to some outer stimulus. For example, when we feel physically threatened, we may respond with a "fight, flight, or freeze" response. These responses are natural to all living creatures. We all have basic survival instincts built into us. Even flies don't want to be swatted—so they fly away if they can. What we need to recognize, however, is that *all* emotions are just patterns of energy created within us as a response to some stimulus—not just the ones that cause fight, flight or freeze responses.

When you realize this, it can really open your mind to a new way of thinking about emotions—many of which you may feel are "responsible" for your anxiety. You see, as energy, different emotions simply have different vibrational patterns to them. This is how we are able to distinguish between them. We then *label* them according to the particular sensation we experience.[4] [5] Thus we say "fear," "sadness," "anger," "anxiety," and so forth. This is because we inhabit the verbal world, and need some way to communicate our experiences with others.

But contrary to common belief, feelings are not *mental experiences.* They really can't be explained in a meaningful way— they can only be experienced, as energy. Of course, your mind may be running wild with all kinds of attempts to explain the emotion, to figure it out, how to get rid of it, how you're a victim of it, and so forth. But these are just thoughts or stories, conjured up in an attempt to "explain" the very fundamental human experience of emotional energy in your body. They are not the emotion itself.

It is very important to grasp this concept, because as you'll see, the techniques you'll soon be using to Vaporize Your Anxiety are based on the idea that feelings are just energy. To move beyond anxiety, you must simply be willing to experience that energy fully.

---

4 Institute of HeartMath, an organization that investigates emotional energy and intuitive development.

5 Power vs. Force: The Hidden Determinants of Human Behavior, by David R. Hawkins, MD, Ph.D.

chapter 3

Understanding the Basis of Preverbal Conditioning

In order to understand how preverbal conditioning affects us, it will be useful to take a look at the basic structure of all human experiences. Every human experience is composed of three fundamental components: The person having the experience, or the *experiencer*, the *object of experience*, and the *process of experiencing*. For example, if you take a bite of a strawberry, you are the experiencer, the strawberry is the experience, and your senses—in this case, taste, touch, smell, sight and even hearing (slurp!)—represent the process of experiencing. Together, these three comprise our experiences.

The Three Aspects of Human Awareness

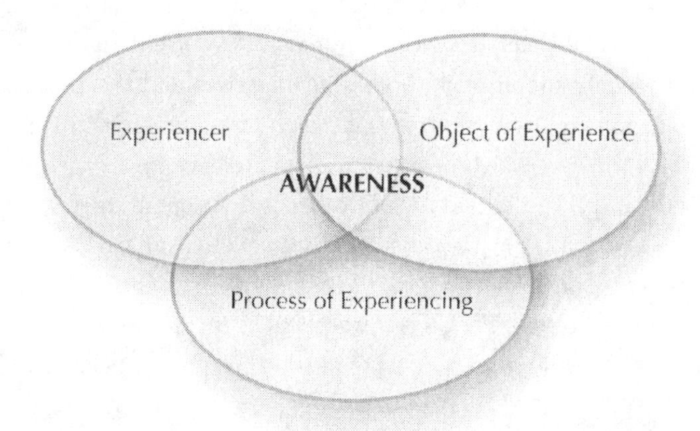

As we've discussed, when we are very young we have experiences that are too much for our delicate systems to process. Our mechanisms of experiencing are not yet developed enough to handle many of our experiences prior to developing language. So as a result, we tend to become inappropriately identified with a mistaken interpretation of one or more of the three components of experience. And this is where problems begin.

If we identify too strongly with the object of our experience, we tend to develop the sense that some crucial part of ourselves is missing. If we identify too strongly with our notions of who we think we are (the experiencer), we tend to develop the sense that we are our ego. If we identify too strongly with the process of experiencing, we will often end up being easily overwhelmed and afraid to feel things fully. As the diagram on the facing page shows, identifying too strongly with any one of the three aspects keeps us from experiencing a sense of being whole, and of feeling things fully. We will be cut off from *Pure Awareness.*[6]

Of course, like most things in life, there is considerable flow between these three modes of experience. Often we experience two simultaneously. For example, if we tend to identify strongly both with ourselves and with the object of our experience, we end up feeling frustration, because we are completely identified with our ego and at the same time feel strongly that some part of ourselves is missing. If we identify too strongly both with ourselves and the process of experiencing, we end up feeling like we're in constant struggle, because the ego, which demands that its presence be recognized, is battling against the temptation to become absent in the face of strong emotions. If, on the other hand, we tend to over-identify with the object of our experience and the process of experiencing, we can feel terribly isolated, since we at once feel as though some part of ourselves is not there and we feel terrified of being overwhelmed.

6 Pure Awareness is the title of my first book. I have dedicated a short section to a basic explanation of the concept in Chapter 11 of this book. You can download the full E-book for free at www.pureawarenessbook.com

The Origin of Problems

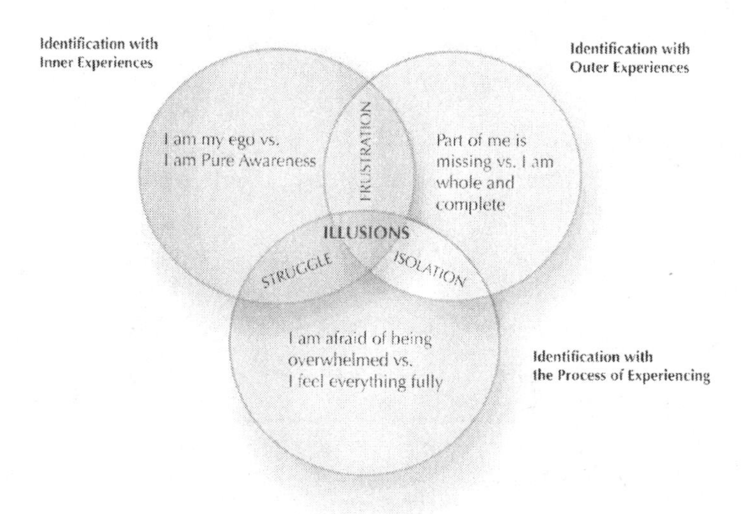

If you've been suffering from anxiety, you may have identified with some of the feelings I described in the last paragraph. And whether you have become identified with one, two or all three of these components of human experience, you'll tend to remain stuck, unable to become truly aware of the wholeness of your experiences. You'll suffer under illusions, and will often be helpless to change things. In fact, that feeling of helplessness is one of the hallmarks of anxiety. The thing is, unless you confront and resolve these unseen bugs in your inner human software and find ways to "debug" yourself, you will continue to live inside the severe limitations that these feeling-level decisions create. But that is precisely what *Vaporize Your Anxiety* is about. The breakthrough techniques you'll find in this book will allow you once and for all to self-heal the unresolved, often intense emotional energy that you've been holding in your body and begin—perhaps for the first time—to enjoy the fullness of human experience, free from anxiety, and open to all that life has to offer.

chapter 4

The ACE Study & The Inability to Self-Heal Emotional Pain

In the summer of 2005, I read about a scientific study called the Adverse Childhood Experiences (ACE) Study, which was described in an article entitled "The Relation Between Adverse Childhood Experiences and Adult Health: Turning Gold into Lead," by Vincent J. Felitti, M.D.[7]

At the time, Dr. Felitti was head of the department of Preventive Medicine at Kaiser Permanente in San Diego. His co-researcher for the study was Dr. Robert Anda of the Center for Disease Control. This major study, which involved 17,421 adult Kaiser Health Plan members, reveals a powerful relationship between, on the one hand, traumatic childhood experiences, and on the other, adult physical and emotional health, major illness, and even early death.

The ACE Pyramid, showing the progression from Adverse Childhood Experiences to Early Death.

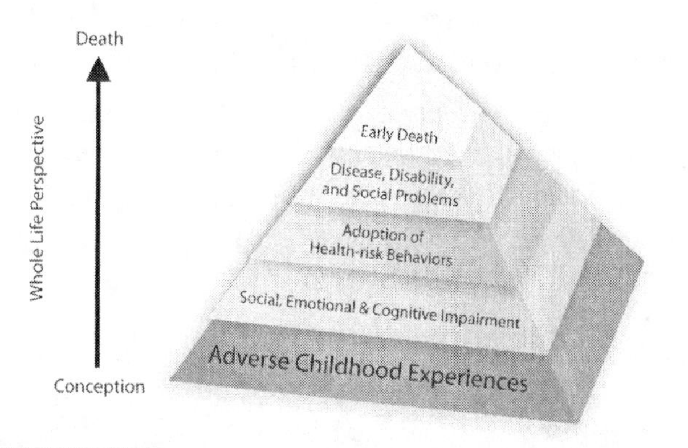

7 The Permanente Journal, Kaiser Permanente, Winter 2002, Vol. 6, No. 1. http://xnet.kp.org/permanentejournal/winter02/goldtolead.html

The ACE Pyramid represents the conceptual framework for the study. In the 1980s and early 1990s, information about risk factors for disease had been widely researched and merged into public education and prevention programs. It became clear that many risk factors—such as smoking, alcohol abuse, and sexual behaviors that put people at risk for certain diseases—were not randomly distributed in the population. In fact, it was known that risk factors for many chronic diseases tended to cluster—that is, persons who had one risk factor tended to have one or more others.

The ACE study was designed to generate data that would help answer the question: "If risk factors for disease, disability, and early mortality are not randomly distributed, what influences precede the adoption or development of them?" This data would then provide previously unavailable scientific information that could be used to develop more effective prevention programs. By taking a whole-life perspective, the ACE Study uncovered how childhood stressors are strongly related to the development and prevalence of risk factors for disease and social well being, throughout the human lifespan.[8]

These findings are important not only from a medical perspective. They also provide social and economic insights into how we become what we are as individuals and as a nation. As we struggle to understand mental and physical health crises that go beyond what even seems conceivable in a "developed" country, the ACE Study becomes a key piece of the puzzle. It helps to explain not only the prevalence of these conditions, but their almost eerie persistence in our culture (recall the statistics on anxiety cited at the beginning of Chapter 1),

8 Adapted from Adverse Childhood Experiences Study, http://www.cdc.gov/nccdphp/ace/pyramid.htm.

in spite of medical services that are considered by many to be the most advanced anywhere in the world. And indeed, the time factors in the study make it clear (the average age of participants was 57) that time did *not* heal many common adverse childhood experiences among a large population of middle-aged, middle-class Americans. So it turns out that unresolved emotional pain and trauma is not only the underlying cause of a broad range of psychological and physical health problems, but even worse, many people do not and cannot "just get over it" naturally, with the passing of time.

Among the study's findings was the discovery that a huge number of adult conditions—including heart disease, diabetes, obesity, alcoholism, hepatitis, fractures, occupational health, and job performance—are all directly associated with childhood traumas. The study also found a strong correlation with mental and emotional problems such as anxiety and depression. And one rather shocking discovery was that the number of *distinct categories* of childhood traumas someone endured has a direct correlation with the rate of prescriptions for psychotropic drugs. In other words, the more varied, severe, and repeated the childhood traumas, the more likely that someone will suffer from conditions requiring these drugs, like anxiety and depression.[9]

Of course, the ACE Study merely confirms what many of us who work in the healing arts have known intuitively for a long time: emotional problems are often the sinister force behind not only psychological problems, but physiological ones as well. The graded correlations (that is, more childhood trauma equals a higher incidence of adult physical and mental health problems) of the ACE Study, with its large

9 The ACE Study developed an "ACE Score" by grouping adverse childhood experiences into eight general categories and then noting the number of distinct categories each participant had been exposed to. The categories were: (1) recurrent physical abuse; (2) recurrent emotional abuse; (3) sexual abuse; (4) living with an alcoholic person or a drug user; (5) family member in prison; (6) family member chronically depressed, mentally ill, or suicidal; (7) mother treated violently; (8) parents separated, divorced, or in some way absent during childhood. There was a direct, graded correlation between Ace Score and adult pharmacy costs, number of doctor office visits, emergency department use, hospitalization, and death.

population and high statistical significance, finally prove what we have suspected to be true all along. And while this may be depressing news to the medical industry, with its reliance on the treatment of symptoms, it is in fact heartening to those of us working in the field of Human Software Engineering.

The reason is this: While the ACE Study demonstrates that adult health risks can be the direct result of childhood trauma, and proves that the emotional fallout from these traumas is highly resistant to self-healing, it fails to address one extremely important point: Why? That is, *why* are these adverse experiences so resistant to self-healing? After all, if you cut your finger, the finger will heal in a week. If you break your leg, the pain may be intense, and the recovery time may be a month or more. But eventually, the pain subsides, the bone heals, and for all intents and purposes, you're "over it."

If the body is in many cases so good at healing itself, why is this not the case with the mental/emotional trauma of these adverse childhood experiences? The results of the ACE Study make it clear that new methods are needed for resolving the resistance to self-healing, so that the long-term impact of these childhood traumas can be mitigated, but it does not answer, in effect, the "million dollar question."

The solution to this riddle may be simpler than it first appears, and this is why we in the field of Human Software Engineering can be heartened by the results of the ACE Study. If one considers that the Core Dynamics model of preverbal conditioning can explain how we unwittingly create the conditions that cause us to resist healing from emotionally traumatic events, it is certainly plausible that this preverbal conditioning can create a kind of preliminary layer in the ACE pyramid that comes before the traumas and actually causes the inability to self-heal. Without the layer of preverbal conditioning, the adverse childhood experiences would be much like breaking your leg—painful, even traumatic, but ultimately healed by good care and the passage of time.

In the revised version of the ACE pyramid on the next page, a "base layer" has been added. My experience shows that preverbal conditioning, which we have identified as the key to many of our emotional difficulties in adult life, also preconditions us to resist healing from the kinds of adverse childhood experiences that are detailed in the ACE Study. It sets us up to try to escape from the pain created by the residual effects of unresolved traumas rather than heal them. The startling piece of information the ACE Study adds to my own work is the possibility that this same preverbal conditioning might actually be putting our health at risk, and even cause early death. That is why I feel so heartened by the findings of the ACE Study. As the general public becomes aware that traumas resistant to self-healing can become the source of adult health risks, they will become more open to discovering ways to overcome that resistance, and truly heal their childhood traumas.

Needless to say, what I learned from the ACE Study made me feel that it was urgent to get my message out. If you are suffering from anxiety and you exhibit other destructive or escape-type behaviors, you have probably experienced more than one of the categories of adverse childhood experiences listed in the study. Using the techniques in Part II of this book to vaporize your anxiety may therefore remove the need for the other behaviors and have a kind of very positive "domino effect" on your life.

Core Dynamics Pyramid

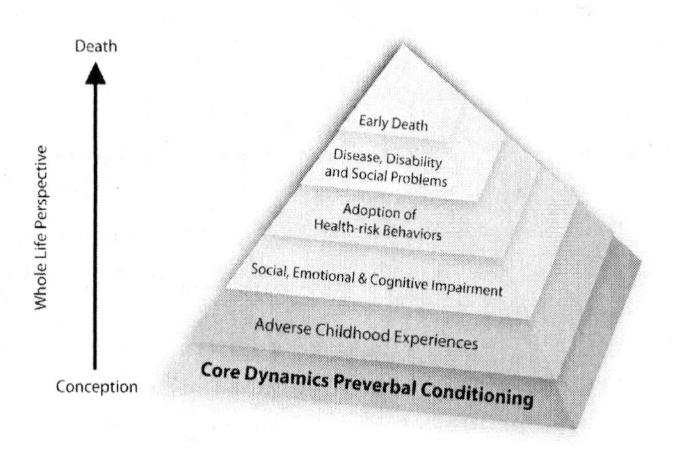

After reading Dr. Felitti's article on the Kaiser-Permanente website, I contacted him immediately. He agreed to meet with me so that we could discuss the possible relationship between the ACE Study and the work that I had been doing with Human Software Engineering. In a subsequent meeting, he kindly allowed me to interview him about the ACE Study. The video of our interview is available in the Resources Section of the Vaporize Your Anxiety website. You can watch it there, and check out all the other helpful resources at: **www.VaporizeYourAnxiety.com/resources.html**

chapter 5

The 12 Core Dynamics of Common Problems

Up to this point, we've focused on the concept of pre-verbal conditioning and feeling-level decisions, without discussing the nature and specific effects of those decisions. There are twelve essential forms of preverbal conditioning that, when taken together, form what I call "The Core Dynamics of Common Problems." The Core Dynamics are a set of penetrating insights about the nature of preverbal human conditioning. They were discovered over many years of inquiry and research while developing the field of Human Software Engineering. They are the basis for a new way of understanding the ways in which our past emotional conflicts continue to limit our present life (that is, if left unresolved).

The Core Dynamics of Common Problems

If you are already familiar with my work, you have probably heard the term "Core Dynamics" before. A big part of my work is as a teacher and trainer of life coaches, who can become certified "Core Dynamics Coaches" through my company, Great Life Coaching. Core Dynamics coaches tend to be very much in demand because what they offer is so different from what traditional life coaches offer. I am thrilled to say that our unique community of coaches is growing daily, making these insights available to people around the world that continue to struggle unnecessarily.

Now, you may be wondering why I'm telling you all this. The reason is that there can often be some confusion about Core Dynamics until you've actually experienced Core Dynamics Coaching. I want to try to be clear about what they are, and what they're not, so you really understand them. The Core Dynamics are a set of conditioned responses under whose invisible influence almost all of us operate, without even knowing it. That's why I call them The Core Dynamics of *Common Problems*. Core Dynamics coaching is not, as some people mistakenly believe, a way to "learn the Core Dynamics." Rather, it is a way to approach personal growth by giving people experiences of living *without* the influence of the Core Dynamics. We support people in becoming free of them, so that they can live from a place of authenticity and true freedom.

Each Core Dynamic is the expression of one of those "feeling-level decisions" we made when we were very young. As we've discussed, these decisions were not made with words—they were preverbal and precognitive. When we grow up and acquire verbal and cognitive skills, we forget that we made these powerful feeling-level decisions, such as the decision to do our best to avoid being emotionally overwhelmed by shutting down our access to our own innate capacity to feel. So we are left with a series of limiting ideas and behaviors that are entrenched and unassailable through therapy.

What the whole thing comes down to, however, is a conditioned response that keeps us in a perpetual state of underused potential.

In the case of anxiety, we have become especially good at avoiding fully feeling (and thus resolving) the fear that is at its root. If you refer to the diagram above, you'll see the central Core Dynamic called "Resisting Feeling Things Fully." I have found in my work that this is the primary core dynamic anxiety sufferers are dealing with. The Core Dynamic of Resisting Feeling Things Fully tends to create people who become very "skilled" at this emotional-overwhelm-avoidance strategy. Unfortunately, this skill has also kept us in the perpetual low-grade experience that we call anxiety. And until we make some major breakthroughs around this fundamental way that we have learned to function, we will typically stay stuck in it.

Debugging the Core Dynamics of Human Conditioning

The fundamental breakthrough we need to make, then, is to let go of our conditioned avoidance response, and truly make the decision to feel things fully. In fact, in part two of this book, you'll learn a technique called "Feeling into the Core of the Energy of the Feeling." Wow—that's a mouthful! But as you'll see when you begin using it, it is really just an accurate, non-technical description of a very elegant, simple, and powerful way to liberate yourself from the grip of emotion.

As I described in Chapter 2, when we're cut off from our innate capacity to feel things fully, we tend to leave the experience of intense feelings incomplete. Carrying around these accumulated incomplete emotional experiences creates "emotional baggage"—the old, unresolved, painfully intense feelings that we travel with every day, often without even knowing it. Most of us have *suitcases* full of emotional pain we carry around with us, unaware that we could just... toss it out. We may be able to successfully distract ourselves from these feelings for a while—even, as I've suggested, by getting really good at being anxious!—but whenever life settles down for a few moments, there they are, pressing up to the surface, wanting to be felt and healed.

People become resigned to this state, and assume that this must just be "how life is." Think about it: so many of us live with anxiety, nervousness, and depression on a *daily basis.* And we think it's normal. Or if we don't, we assume there's no alternative that doesn't involve medication. Of course, this is a logical assumption, given the nearly universal beliefs that we can't handle "too much emotion." (That's okay—we can just take a pill!) This belief really *feels as if it's true,* because we've spent our whole lives conditioned to resist feeling things fully. So it's hard to believe it could be otherwise. But the truth is, *it's not the truth!*

Burden of Baggage

The good news is that you *can* handle all the emotions you will ever encounter, in their complete and unadulterated intensity. As we discussed earlier, neuro-scientific research has proven that as adults we have acquired all the spindle cells necessary to process our emotions, even the painful and terrifying ones. The problem is, we're still operating based on a three year-old's unwitting decision to avoid feeling things fully.

In other words, we have the right "hardware," but our "software" or "operating system" is so full of bugs that we can't handle robust emotional experiences. It's kind of like having a modern computer with tons of memory and a powerful processor, but running on an operating system from 1985. You can keep expanding the memory and buying faster processors, but until you update the operating system, you'll never be able to realize the computer's true potential. And when you finally *do* update the operating system and get rid of those bugs, all of a sudden, your computer runs like a dream.

Likewise, when our lives are being run by the Core Dynamics, no amount of intellectually advanced, streamlined thinking can get us out from under their spell. Instead, our inner human software operating system needs to be upgraded. We need to upgrade from a state in which we are operating on the fear of being overwhelmed to a state of being in which we can access our innate, if unused, capacity to feel. This will allow us to learn how to experience the energy of emotions in our body to completion, without the fear of being overwhelmed by them.

No More Freezes!

Have you ever noticed that anxiety has the effect of making you feel like you can't take action—even if you know exactly what action you should take? When anxiety is intense, it's almost like you freeze. We all know what it's like when our computer freezes, right? Well, it's very much the same with anxiety. When you're plagued by the human software bugs that create anxiety, you simply get stuck, and often the only way to get past it is to "shut down" and "restart." The problem with that strategy is that when you restart, the problem is still there, waiting to show up (in the form of anxiety) when confronted with a triggering experience.

What you will experience in the second half of this book, however, is a way to debug your inner software so that you won't "freeze" when you encounter anxiety-triggering situations. You will literally upgrade your inner human software by learning to feel things completely. You will learn how to join the three components of every human experience—the experiencer, the object experienced, and the process of experiencing—so that you can operate from a state of integration and wholeness. As you will see, it is not only possible to be completely free from anxiety; it's much easier than you think. I invite you, then, to come along as we dive into the practical application of the anxiety vaporizing techniques that I've developed. You're closer than you think to freedom from anxiety!

chapter 6

Is This a Form of Therapy?

Soon we'll be moving into the second half of the book, where I outline the practical application of the techniques we've been discussing, and give you a roadmap for Vaporizing Your Anxiety. But before we get there, I feel I should address one question I get a lot: Are the techniques described in this book a form of therapy? My response is that while they have a wonderfully therapeutic effect, they are in fact a form of *training*. Training, that is, in how to access and effectively utilize your previously underutilized capacity to feel—a phenomenon we discussed in Chapter 2. Remember, you already have this innate capability. You just haven't learned to use it yet.

This phenomenon actually has some intriguing similarities with the history and evolution of reading. Language based on an alphabet rather than symbols began to evolve in the Middle East about 3800 years ago. (It was "perfected" by the Greeks about 2500 years ago.) This was a major advance from the earlier Egyptian method of using hieroglyphics or pictures to represent spoken words. It standardized language and enabled people to "write" and "read," rather than simply convey and receive information based on pictures. However, for most of its history, reading was done orally—by speaking the sounds of the letters and words out loud. In fact, speaking was necessary for understanding the meaning of words and sentences. The ability to read silently didn't evolve until about the 15th Century, and only became the norm in the 19th Century.

Imagine the amazement of people when they first encountered someone who was able to read words only inside their heads, and know their meaning—without speaking them out loud. It must have seemed like a miracle! And yet now we take silent reading for granted. In fact, it's far more common than reading out loud. The truth is, human beings had the ability to read silently all along, but just didn't know they had it.

If you've ever watched a child learning to read, you've actually witnessed something quite similar on a small scale. Most children can't read silently at first. They need to sound out each word. Strangely though, once they get the hang of it, they usually continue to read out loud. It's only once someone tells them that it's possible to read to themselves that they actually start doing it. They always had this innate ability, they just didn't know it.

Likewise, we all have the innate ability to feel things fully. But much like the period before reading silently became the norm, we're now living in an era of human development in which our ability to access and use our innate ability to feel has been limited by our conditioning.

I would suggest that many of the problems people have are really caused by this inability to process their emotions. Perhaps once we become competent at doing this it will render the notion that we need therapy to resolve our problems obsolete. That's not to say that it won't take well-trained guides to help those who have severe issues that go beyond what you can learn from a book. And indeed, for people with severe psychological conditions, therapy may be necessary. But so called "normal" people—in other words, most of us—may only need to learn how to access and use their natural capabilities that have just lain dormant up until now.

So, again: Is this a form of therapy? I think not. It is training in how to use formerly underutilized parts of our natural abilities. Like with physical training (and unlike therapy), you must practice until you get good. But I assure you that if you are capable of feeling, you too can clean up your inner landscape, overcome the conditioning that makes you resistant to feeling, and Vaporize Your Anxiety once and for all.

Part II
The Solution

chapter 7

Resolving the Fear at the CORE of Your Anxiety

An Introduction to the CORE Technique

"I've been using the CORE Technique and it's just been amazing for me. Even when I've been anxious about things like money and bills I'm able to come out of the anxiety and fear so that I can just deal with everything so much better. It brings me back to a state of centeredness so that I can just do whatever needs to be done without staying caught up in the drama. I have thanked God everyday for the CORE Technique. It is awesome and I am so grateful!

– Barbara Whorley - Business Coach/Consultant/Speaker
Capo Beach, CA

The CORE Technique is an elegant and incredibly powerful technique that I have developed over the last 20 years. It is the main tool you'll be using to vaporize your anxiety. The CORE Technique is extremely effective for resolving the kind of childhood emotional traumas that are typically at the root of anxiety. Mastering this technique, which can be accomplished simply by practicing it often, will enable you not only to vaporize your anxiety, but also to live in the richness of your emotional experiences without fear of being overwhelmed.

CORE stands for "Center of Remaining Energy." As I talked about earlier, the energy of unresolved emotional experiences tends to undermine our adult lives. The key thing to keep in mind here is the idea these emotional experiences are just energy. The CORE technique involves going inside to the center of the energy that's being held in the body, and experiencing it fully. This is the opposite of what we're conditioned to do. We're conditioned to move away from the energy, because of the Core Dynamic of *Resisting Feeling Things Fully* (see Part I, Chapter 5).

The problem with this, though, is that when you stay out at the edges, or even avoid allowing yourself to experience the energy of the incomplete experience at all, you're actually not avoiding it—you're holding onto it, tightly! As a result, it remains incomplete and becomes a barrier to so many things in life, especially when it comes to being clear about who you really are, what you want in life, and what you should do to achieve these things.

As I mentioned in the introduction, those of us who have anxiety tend not to handle stressful events very well. We often get caught up in fear and anxious feelings and feel like we don't have any control over the process. Minor things—a vague email from a coworker, a little pain somewhere in your body, distressing local news stories—can trigger an onset of anxiety. This can be very disconcerting, both because the anxiety itself is uncomfortable, and because you feel that it's inappropriate to have the reaction you're having.

But the thing to realize is, when something stressful or scary happens, it's usually not only the stress or scariness of the current situation that creates anxiety (although that can certainly be the case). Often, the unresolved emotional pain from previous events is triggered by something stressful in the present, which then in turn triggers an attack of anxiety. Because the previous experiences were never completed, the energy associated with them is archived in the body, just waiting until a new experience triggers the old incompletion and brings it back into awareness. You end up feeling helpless, and afraid.

If certain circumstances trigger your anxiety, you can undoubtedly relate to what I'm talking about here.

However, when you begin to use the CORE Technique to vaporize your anxiety, you are making two very conscious decisions. The first is to stop being the victim of your anxious feelings. You have the ability to master these feelings and move on. This may seem difficult at first but it will get easier the more you do it. Many people who have suffered from anxiety for a long time are highly identified with these feelings of being victimized, and with good reason. But now is the time to shed your skin of victimhood and move into the light of something new and wonderful.

The second decision you're making is to confront your emotions completely. Since anxiety is very uncomfortable, and in some cases even debilitating, my next statement may seem strange, but I assure you, my research and experience helping people resolve their anxiety bears it out. Here it is: in most cases, anxiety is a *strategy* that allows people to avoid something else. In this case, that "something else" is simply some very intense, incomplete emotional energy. Imagine—at some subconscious level, you believe that anxiety is actually *better* than the alternative! The wonderful thing about the CORE Technique, though, is that facing these pockets of intense, incomplete emotional energy in your body is not about dredging up painful memories or telling your most shameful stories to a therapist. It is simply about experiencing and completing the energy from the past that is still held in your body.

You will undoubtedly feel a lot when you begin to do the CORE Technique. As you let go of anxiety, many suppressed emotions are likely to come into your awareness. Some of them may seem to show up with great intensity. It's important to be well prepared for this, or you may not stick with it until the energy of the feelings has been truly completed. But you've chosen to adopt a new strategy of healing—

healing yourself from all the underlying fear and emotional pain. So hang in there—you can handle it!

I feel that it is important to mention something here: If your anxiety seems to be there all the time, you may feel that it's just too much to tackle. Your mind may be racing so much that just calming down enough to do the CORE Technique seems beyond reach. I would like you to consider that the constant presence of this anxiety simply means that you have some fears that are so present and so unresolved that they are always with you. Even if this is the case, you will very likely be able to resolve them using the techniques you are about to learn.

If, however, you try the CORE Technique, but feel as though your present-day fears are too omnipresent to cut through, I would like to encourage you to try the SEE Technique, which is described in Chapter 20. I have found that for some people, starting with the CORE Technique poses too much of a challenge. However, many of these people have wonderful success with the SEE Technique, which allows them to immediately extract themselves from being lost inside of the emotion and to quickly access a clam place of inner peace. Afterwards, using the CORE Technique to resolve older emotional pain becomes much easier if that's still needed.

chapter 8

Preparing to learn the CORE Technique

CORE = Center Of Remaining Energy

As I've said, we tend to hold the patterns of incomplete experiences in our bodies. These incomplete experiences are made of energy, and the field of this energy typically feels rather like a hurricane. The intensity of the energy is stronger at the center and weaker at the edges.

Allowing yourself to go to the core— to the most intense part of the energy of an incomplete emotional experience—is an exhilarating experience. It is sort of like sky diving right into the eye of a hurricane. As you move toward the center, it gets more and more intense, but when you arrive at the true center, you suddenly encounter stillness. You discover that the safest and easiest place to focus your attention is in fact the very center—the most intense part of the energy of the feeling.

As it turns out, the way ***OUT*** of the anxiety and fear is actually... ***IN***.

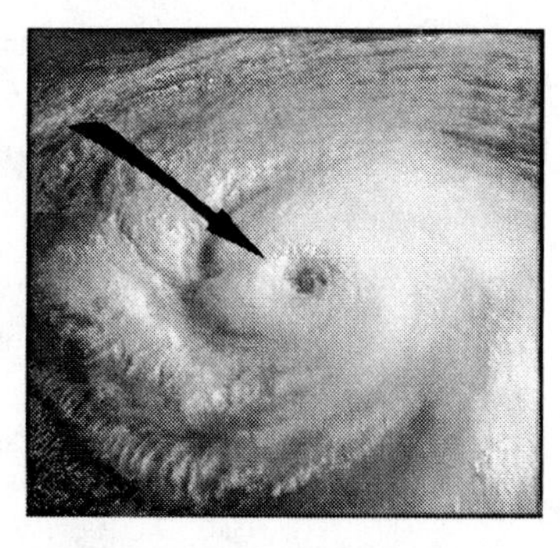

However, there are often layers of an incomplete emotional experience, each stacked on top of the others. As you dive down into the core of the energy, it seems to be gone, but then you find another layer of the incomplete experience. In fact, sometimes there can be several layers, each with a different quality of feeling. That's just fine: when you encounter a new layer, you simply locate the core of the new layer and dive down into it.

I really need to stress that this is not at all uncommon. In fact, I had this exact experience the first several times I did the CORE Technique. I remember clearly, on one occasion, the first layer was anger. When I had felt into the core of the anger so thoroughly that there wasn't any anger left, I found a feeling of hurt underneath. Again I felt down into the energy of the feeling of hurt until there was nothing left to feel. Under that there was deep sadness. And beyond that, a feeling of being alone and isolated. But when I had felt into the most intense part of each of these layers of unresolved feelings, I finally "came out the bottom," and there was nothing left at all. It was like the clouds burning off in the morning sun. Everything just opened up and expanded, and I was in a clear experience of *Pure Awareness.* So remember: if there are layers of feelings stacked on top of each other, just find the center of each one in turn and feel down into them until there is nothing left to feel.

Another thing to be aware of is that sometimes the layers of an incomplete emotional experience have been stored in several different places on your "internal hard drive" (your body). You may find that when the energy of one layer seems to be fading away, the energy of another layer will start to be experienced in another part of your body. Again, this is completely normal. Whether there are several layers or just one, and whether the layers are in one location or in several, when you feel your way down into the core of the most intense part of the energy you will eventually find... nothing. And this, believe it or not, is really what we're after: the "nothingness" out of which we create all of our experiences – even the reactions to our emotions that we're now completing.

Interestingly, this nothingness from which the energy of the reaction was created corresponds very well to what is called the "Unified Field" in quantum physics. Unified Field theory holds that various forces are really manifestations of one larger unifying principle. So when you complete the experience of the energy of the reaction that's been stored, you are directly experiencing the quantum field from which the energy of the experience had manifested.

Everyone who has anxiety would like to be free of it. Otherwise, there would be no need for this book. You need a realistic strategy for dealing with anxiety causing situations so that you can avoid slipping back into a pattern that makes you a victim of your emotional reactions. One strategy immediately available to you is to begin practicing the CORE Technique right away, so that you'll quickly become good at it. By doing this, you'll quickly gain the confidence that comes with knowing that *you can really feel any emotion fully* without become victimized by it. You'll get so used to using the CORE Technique that as soon as you feel yourself slipping into an anxious state, your reflex will be to do the technique, rather than to go into a true state of anxiety.

If you've been suffering from Anxiety for some time, you have undoubtedly gotten pretty good at dancing around the edges of the energy of unresolved fears. Once you begin using the CORE Technique, you may find a suitcase or two filled with them. You may need to do the CORE Technique many times, because there are likely to be many patterns of energy of fears that haven't been completed. Then again, maybe you just have one big fear that you need to resolve. In either case, using the CORE technique will allow you to vaporize the energy of the fear. Each time you complete an incomplete experience of one of the fears at the root of your anxiety you'll notice that that situation doesn't trigger anxious feelings any more.

Although reading about and understanding these concepts are important steps, the CORE Technique is really about having an *experience*. It is a very special, very particular kind of experience. To *get it* you need to *do it*. So I'd like to invite you to listen to some examples of people being guided through the CORE Technique, which I have recorded specially for readers of this book. After listening to these recordings, I'll give you a step-by-step description of how to do it. Just visit **www.VaporizeYourAnxiety.com/resources.html** and you'll be able to listen to the recordings right on the website, or download them to play on your computer or mp3 player.

chapter 9

Making your List

Welcome back!

Now that you've heard examples of people being guided through the CORE Technique, you can learn how to do it yourself. The best way to start this process is by making a list of the things that make you anxious. If you are at all like me, when you read a book and the author gives you some exercise to do you may not feel like doing it. Please don't skip this step! It's so important because in order to learn the CORE Technique you're going to have to get in touch with the feelings that are the real core of your anxiety. This is an essential part of being able to learn and do the CORE Technique effectively.

So go ahead and get a piece of paper and write down at least a few of the things that you are anxious about. If you are anxious all the time, this may still be a useful exercise and it probably means there may be one thing or just a few big things that are driving your anxiety. Or it may be that there are a whole bunch of them. Either way, making the list is probably going to be useful. So please do that now. If you'd like, you can go to **www.vaporizeyouranxiety.com/resources.html** and download a worksheet that will help you with this exercise. But if you're not at your computer, don't let that hold you back—a regular piece of paper and pen will do just fine!

If you're having trouble getting started, here are some things that others have said make them anxious. See if you can relate to any of these:

"My employer has been laying people off and even though my job hasn't been affected yet, the rumor going around the office is that there will be more layoffs. I really worry that I'll be one of the next ones to get that pink slip."

"I have to give a presentation to a group of people I've never met. I know my topic, but I have bad stage fright, and it's always worse when I don't know anyone in the audience. I'm concerned about how they are going to respond to me, and I'm worried I'll look ridiculous."

"My teenage daughter has been out all night, and she didn't tell me that this was going to happen. It's 3:00 AM and she didn't take her cell phone with her."

"Two months ago I had a car accident, and I can't seem to shake it. I'm recovered physically, but I'm terrified to drive."

"I was mugged last month, and it really scared me. I wasn't hurt or anything, but even though I know it's not rational, I just don't feel safe walking around by myself."

"I was raped several years ago. I have had great counseling, and the person who did it is in jail, but I can't get over it. I'm afraid it will happen again."

"I was in an emotionally abusive relationship for two years. It's over now, but every time I meet someone new, I get so scared that it will happen again. I really want to start a new relationship, but I feel frozen."

"One of my close coworkers was caught embezzling from our company. I had nothing to do with it, but I'm afraid I'll be guilty by association."

"I was living in San Francisco when the earthquake hit in 1989. I don't live anywhere near a fault line now, but I'm still scared. I hold my breath every time I drive over a bridge."

"I have a lot of nightmares and scary thoughts. Sometimes I'm scared to go to sleep at night."

"Every year, on the anniversary of the day I was attacked, I get so anxious I can hardly move."

"Last year, out of the blue, my best man died suddenly—only three years after my wedding. He was in great health. I'm afraid something like that will happen to me."

"I'm in a very dysfunctional, co-dependent relationship. I know what's wrong with it, but I'm afraid I don't have the willpower to end it. So I walk around anxious all the time."

"I'm in serious debt. I've tried so many things, and nothing helps. I think bankruptcy may be the only way out, but I'm scared that if I declare bankruptcy I'll be ostracized by everyone I know. I just feel frozen—I have no idea what to do."

"I just heard the report on CNN about that terrorist attack, and I'm afraid we're next."

You may have your own variations of these themes, or have completely different triggering situations in your life. Either way, take just 5 or 10 minutes to make your list (you can feel free to add to it at any time, of course). Try to be as specific as possible. For example, don't write, "Meeting new people makes me anxious." Instead, say something like, "When I met that nice single guy my friends invited to dinner, I got so anxious. It was like I couldn't even speak. It's weird, because I am smart and funny, and he obviously thought I was attractive. I don't know, I just froze."

It's important to include as much detail as possible about these triggering situations, because that way, you'll really be able to hone in on the *precise* energy of the feeling in your body that is associated with the event. That is the key to success with the CORE Technique.

chapter 10

Practice: Using the CORE Technique to Vaporize Your Anxiety

You are now ready to begin. You've learned what the CORE Technique is by reading Chapter 2 and listening to the recordings on our website. You've made your list of anxiety-triggering situations, being as specific as possible.

To do the exercise below, I recommend that you find someone you're comfortable with and go through the exercise with this person guiding you. The best kind of person for this is a close friend or a spouse, someone you trust and who is willing to be there for you without judgment, just to help. Practicing the CORE Technique with someone guiding you through it the first few times will make it easier to learn than simply attempting to do it yourself.

One thing to keep in mind: It is often difficult to pinpoint the location in your body where you experience the physical sensation of anxiety. Anxious feelings tend to either feel like they're "everywhere," or "enveloping" your body. You may even feel like you're being consumed by the energy. Because this is often the case, there is a special way of doing the CORE Technique when using it specifically to resolve the underlying incompletions that cause anxiety. I developed this variation of the CORE Technique because anxiety sufferers often have a hard time finding the place in their bodies where the energy of the anxiety is held, and this is very important for the CORE Technique to work. Normally, when practicing the CORE Technique, the very first question is something along the lines of "Where do you feel the energy in your body?" But after working with many people who suffer from anxiety, I began to realize that this was often too much of a challenge for them. So we begin with a preliminary step.

To start off, we have to bring your attention to the field of energy of the anxiety. This alone can be challenging, because it means that you have to allow yourself to feel the anxious feeling. Now, you may have anxious feelings all the time or you may only feel anxious under certain circumstances. If you feel anxious all the time then it shouldn't take much to notice the feeling of anxiety. If you only get anxious about certain things, it should still be pretty easy to get in touch with feeling anxious: Just allow yourself to think about one of the situations or circumstances that make you anxious from your list. Whether you feel anxious all the time or just under certain circumstances the idea is to start by simply allowing yourself to feel the entire feeling of the anxious energy.

Instructions for the person reading:

Read the bold sections in quotation marks (" ") out loud and read the italicized sections silently. Start here:

"**Please sit comfortably and close your eyes.**"

Wait for a few moments, then say:

"**Allow yourself to feel the entire feeling of the field of the energy of the anxiety. Just let yourself be fully present and feel the whole of its energy.**"

Pause here for a moment before continuing.

"You may start to gradually notice that in the field of energy there is an area where it is more concentrated, more condensed."

Pause

"It will usually tend to be toward the center of the body somewhere, in your chest, solar plexus, or belly (but it could be anywhere)."

Pause

"It may take a little while of allowing yourself to feel the entire field of the energy of the anxious feeling before you will begin to notice this more condensed area within the field of the energy, so just take your time."

Pause

"When you do notice the area that is more condensed—maybe somewhere towards the center of your body—you can let me know by just nodding or say OK."

(Pause and let them be with the experience. When they either nod or say OK you can continue reading.)

"Now that you can feel the area of the energy that is more concentrated or condensed, where in your body do you feel it?"

They will say where they feel it or gesture to an area in the chest or stomach or throat or somewhere. Then say:

"If you allow yourself to, you can sense in that field of energy that there is an area where it is even more intense than it is elsewhere. Can you sense that?"

They will typically acknowledge this with a nod or a yes. If not you can tell them to just allow themselves to feel the field of the energy for a little while and see if after a time they notice that there is an area that is more intense than elsewhere. In a short time they will tend to say yes. At that point, say:

"Now allow yourself to let your awareness go right into the center of the most intense part of the energy of the sensation."

Pause

"Can you do that?"

Pause—(get acknowledgment)

"Okay, go ahead and continue."

Now... WAIT until you have a sense that it's appropriate to speak again. This will range from less than a minute to a minute or two or even more. Then slowly and gently say:

"Usually one of three things happens. Sometimes the sensation will become more intense at first as you haven't been allowing yourself to feel it fully. Sometimes it will seem to stay the same for a time. And sometimes it may start to fade away or soften. Is one of these things happening?"

Typically they will nod or say yes. If they don't volunteer anything you can ask:

"Which one of these are you experiencing?"

There are three possible responses -

It's getting more intense.

It seems to be staying the same.

It seems to be fading away or becoming softer/less intense.

For either #1 or #2 you can then say:

"OK, simply continue to allow your awareness to feel right into the center of the most intense part of the energy of the sensation."

Then give them some time to do that.

For #3—fading away/becoming softer or less intense—say:

"Now bring your awareness in closer to whatever is left of the sensation, again find the center of intensity of the remaining energy, and again allow yourself to feel down into it, just experiencing the essence of the energy."

"The idea is to feel down into the energy of the sensation so thoroughly that there is nothing left to feel."

Give them some time to do this. Then check in again with them to see what is happening. You can say:

"How's it going?"

They may have had some visual experience or the energy they are sensing may have moved to a different place. They may have completed the experience and the energy will have dissipated, and there's nothing left. If they say anything other than that what they found in there was nothing, you have to continue to guide them into the core of the energy of the experience.

"Is there any of the sensation of the energy left?"

Or:

"Is there any charge left?"

If they say yes, say:

"Okay, I'd like you to again place your awareness into the center of the most intense part of whatever is left of that energy. We're not looking for insights, just experiencing the energy of an incomplete experience. This is just the process of completing the experience of the energy that has been held in your body. I'd like you to allow yourself to experience it so thoroughly that there is nothing left to experience."

Continue with them in this way. In the vast majority of cases, the person will come out of the grip of the energy of the incomplete experience, and they'll say something like, "It's better," or "It's gone," or "There's nothing there."

Once they realize that there is nothing left and there is no more energy of the sensation, you can now do what is called a "provocation test." This is to make sure that they really fully experienced every bit of the energy of the incomplete emotional experience and there's truly nothing left of it. Say to them:

"Now that it appears to be gone we are going to check to see that it's really complete. So I'd like you to think about the original thing that was causing you to feel anxious."

Give them a moment. Then say:

"Do you still feel anxious?"

Typically, they'll say "No. It's gone." (Don't be surprised if they smile or look relieved.) Then you can say this:

"You are no longer limited by the presence of the energy that was causing these anxious feelings. Your body has been trying to get you to fully feel this energy and complete the experience that was held there. Now it is complete and your body has stopped creating this energy."

"There was an experience of something there that your body needed you to get, not intellectually but experientially. From this place that you're in now, this place of nothingness, you have total freedom of choice. You're in a state of all possibilities where anxiety doesn't exist."

They may have opened their eyes by now, but if they haven't you can invite them to do that now. This is the end of the guidelines for doing the CORE Technique.

You can continue reading the book by yourself now.

Whether you're someone who has been feeling anxious more or less all the time, or just under certain situations, just check to see if that old familiar anxious feeling is still there or not. I'll bet it's not. This process of thinking about the anxiety or the circumstances under which you feel anxious is called a "provocation test." It is designed to help you make sure that you really completed the experience of the energy of that feeling. Sometimes you might still feel something when you think of it again. If you do still feel any of the anxiety, just go back inside and bring your awareness in close to any remaining energy that might still be there. Feel into the core of it so that you complete the experience of whatever is left of it.

And if for any reason your anxiety is not vaporized, then learn the GAP Technique (Chapter 12), which is the basis of the SEE Technique (Chapter 20). Once you have learned those two techniques, you can apply the SEE Technique to any remaining feeling of anxiety. You'll be amazed to find that your feelings of anxiety, which you may have thought would always be with you, have been vaporized in a matter of minutes.

If you're having trouble finding the right person to assist you, or if you'd like the benefit of working with a highly experienced coach, who can guide you through these techniques, visit us at **www.VaporizeYourAnxiety.com/coaches.html**.

Core Dynamics Coaching is very different from conventional life coaching. We believe that the way to access and live from the natural greatness that is already inside of you is to liberate it—by vaporizing the emotional baggage that prevents your natural greatness from shining through. Core Dynamics Coaches go through a rigorous, 6-month training program that includes extensive work with the CORE and the *Pure Awareness* Techniques discussed later in this book. They are also trained to use some very advanced techniques not covered here. At the website, you can browse the Core Dynamics Coach profiles and sign up for a consultation if you'd like. I have seen so many people benefit enormously from working with a coach, so I'd really like to encourage you to give it a try.

chapter 11

Pure Awareness

Now that you've had the opportunity to experience the CORE Technique, I'd like to talk briefly about a phenomenon called *Pure Awareness.* You might say that *Pure Awareness* is the life force at the center of my work in the field of Human Software Engineering and Core Dynamics Coaching. In fact, the title of my first book is *Pure Awareness: Five Simple Techniques for Experiencing Your Essential Nature.*

You may have noticed that when you feel down into the energy of the feeling, all the way to completion, there can be a sense of the energy dissipating or dissolving, almost like the fog burning off in the morning sun. As that fog lifts what's left is... nothing. Although there is nothing of the energy of the emotion left to experience, however, this nothingness *itself* has some very special characteristics. If you have already experienced this you know that the nothingness feels expansive, peaceful, calm, awake, lively and soothing.

This is the direct experience of your own awareness. I sometimes call this "awareness of awareness," because there is nothing that you are being aware *of* at that moment. Most of the time we are not aware of awareness itself, because our awareness is busy "being aware" of some object of our experience. We are used to experiencing *things* with our awareness, not *nothingness.* But with these techniques, there is no object of experience, just awareness being aware of itself. This very wonderful experience is called *Pure Awareness.* When you do the GAP Technique and the SEE Technique later in the book, you'll see that you arrive in the same place of expansion, peace and calm.

In truth, all the techniques in this book are *Pure Awareness Techniques.* They merely provide you with different ways to reconnect with your Self that are appropriate in different circumstances. They bring you back to a state of being whole and complete. They bring you back to the experience of your essential nature—of who and what you really are.

Admittedly, becoming aware of awareness itself can seem a bit strange at first. But I'm confident you'll discover that the experience of *Pure Awareness* is quite wonderful. These are some of the simplest yet most profoundly useful techniques you may ever learn in your lifetime. You'll find that in *Pure Awareness*, there is no anxiety, no distress, only peace of mind and a deep sense that everything is just fine.

In my experience, the real solution to anxiety is to transcend it—to extract yourself from the grip of emotion, and regain a state of inner peace and happiness. In other words, to cultivate a state in which anxiety simply does not exist and cannot exist. The key thing to remember is that your emotions are not *who you are. Pure Awareness* is who and what all of us *really* are.

Unfortunately, I do not have the space in the present book to give a full presentation of the theory and practice of *Pure Awareness.* But if you'd like to learn about the foundations of my work in Human Software Engineering, which is really what made this book possible, you will find *Pure Awareness* to be invaluable. You can purchase the book at Amazon, or if you'd prefer, you can download the full E-book version for free at **www.pureawarenessbook.com**

Patterns of Energy You May Not Recognize at First

Occasionally, when you feel into something, it may not be obvious at first that what you are feeling is a pattern of energy. A good example of this is the experience of "feeling empty." Emptiness doesn't seem like it would be a feeling or a pattern of energy. It is, though. The trick to catching these patterns of energy that don't even seem like they could be patterns of energy in the first place—and certainly don't seem like "feelings"—is to use the very nature of what they "feel like" as the way to get at them. So if you're feeling empty, allow your awareness to go to the area that feels the MOST empty, much as if you were feeling into the most intense part of the energy of a more "traditional" feeling.

I do want to point out something important, however. Now that you have had the experience of *Pure Awareness*, you may be tempted to equate it with "feeling empty." But there is a subtle (and important) difference between the feeling of *emptiness* and the experience of *Pure Awareness.* When we use the phrase "a feeling of emptiness," there is an implied expectation: something that ought to be there is in fact missing. Most of us have had moments or even long periods in our lives when we were troubled by a sense of emptiness, or lack of motivation, or a lack of enthusiasm for what we were doing in life. This is precisely the kind of feeling that the CORE Technique can be used to resolve.

This "negative" feeling of emptiness is in contrast to the experience of *Pure Awareness*, in which, even though there is no object of experience, the sense of "no-thingness" feels alive and vibrant, and there is a sense of limitless potential, a feeling of pure possibility. Whereas emptiness is an experience of lack, *Pure Awareness* is an experience of abundance. It is in fact the true source of all of our experiences. So if you feel empty, try simply feeling into the most intense part of the emptiness, and beyond it you'll experience the subtle yet powerful shift to *Pure Awareness.*

When doing the CORE Technique, you may encounter other feelings that surprise you, because you wouldn't typically characterize them as feelings. This can be confusing, as with the case of feeling empty. I have found that a very helpful strategy for this situation is simply to think of these quasi-feelings simply as "any experience *other* than *Pure Awareness*." Once you have done the CORE Technique many times you will become quite familiar with *Pure Awareness*. You'll easily be able to tell when something you are experiencing is NOT *Pure Awareness.*

You may also have an expectation that the feelings you encounter, as well as the experience of feeling into them, should be more or less the same every time you practice the CORE Technique. But you'll find that the quality of the energy you encounter doing the CORE Technique can change greatly. In truth, the experience of the energy is often absolutely unique, and this is part of the magic of the techniques, because they open you up to things as they really are—to *yourself* as *you* really are.

chapter 12

When to use the CORE Technique

You can use the CORE Technique any time you feel like you are getting anxious, or for that matter, anytime you feel like you are becoming lost to the grip of emotion. Sometimes a circumstance will trigger the incomplete experience of some fear from the past and you may feel anxious again or you may feel some other uncomfortable feeling. This is the perfect time to remember to use the CORE Technique. Once you are released from the grip of the emotion, you will have reached the state *of Pure Awareness*. You can make the best decisions for your life from this state. So use the CORE Technique any time you feel that anxiety is getting the better of you, and with time you'll discover that you never have to be the victim of anxiety again.

You can use the CORE Technique in two different ways:

Use it on your own to resolve any feelings of anxiety that come up. Those feelings are like a big red flag that can be a helpful reminder that it's time to simply scan your body, find the discomfort that you do not want to feel, and instead, use the CORE Technique. Feel free to experiment with the variations of the CORE Technique I've discussed.

Use it in the context of Core Dynamics Coaching sessions. A trained Core Dynamics Coach will ask you questions to help you identify any "archived" incomplete emotional energy that could also be a source of anxiety. Your Core Dynamics Coach will skillfully inquire about the nature of what is happening inside of you. He or she will gently get you in touch with anything that could be a potential cause of anxiety. Then you'll be carefully guided through the CORE Technique to resolve the basis of your fear and vaporize it.

A few words of additional guidance here may be helpful. Because you are deeply conditioned to want to go away from where the emotional energy is the most intense, you will have an automatic tendency to not use the CORE Technique. It's much more familiar to just stay stuck in the anxiety. This is why so many people have benefited greatly from working with a Core Dynamics coach when beginning this process. It is important to go through the process of using the CORE Technique several times when you are learning it so that you learn to use it instead of collapsing back into old anxious patterns. A coach will help you stay on track. Which leads us to the next important point.

A Common Mistake to Watch Out For

The biggest mistake you can make with the CORE Technique is not to *complete* the experience of the energy that is being held in your body. Sometimes, especially when people are first learning how to do the CORE Technique, they will feel into the feeling for a while and then will back away from it. Instead of completing the experience they will open their eyes and say, "It's better."

What you need to recognize is that this is the result of the same preverbal conditioning—the Core Dynamic of Resisting Feeling Things Fully—that caused you to want to get away from the feelings in the first place! After an initial lessening of intensity, many people who are new to the CORE Technique feel like they want to stop and not feel it any more under these circumstances. So be on the lookout for this pitfall—it is very important to understand the dynamic that's at work here, and to keep feeling deeper into the center of the sensation, until there is literally nothing left to feel.

Many people I've worked with have made the following words into a kind of mantra for doing the CORE Technique. You may wish to write them down and put them somewhere you can see them often.

"Feel into the core of the energy of the feeling completely—so completely there's nothing left to feel."

You can download and print out a full-color version of this quote at

www.VaporizeYourAnxiety.com/resources.html

chapter 13

Doing the MapQuest Thing

Something that can help to ensure that you *do* feel into the core of the energy until there is nothing left to feel is what we've started calling "Doing the MapQuest Thing." When you're using MapQuest and you want to get a closer view, you "click in"—meaning that you click the map, which allows you to zoom in and see a greater level of detail, kind of like increasing the magnification using a telescope or a telephoto lens from an airplane or satellite.

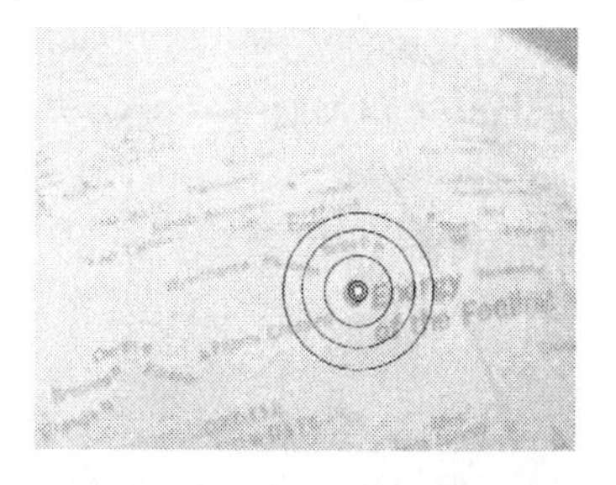

When you are feeling into the core of a feeling and it starts to fade away, rather than succumbing to the tendency to call it a day and stop feeling into it, you can "click in closer," to bring your awareness closer to whatever remains of the energy of the sensation. Again, find the center of the remaining energy and continue to feel down into it. The idea is to keep feeling into the core, then click in closer, feel into the core again, click in closer again, and just keep repeating this exercise until there is literally nothing left to feel.

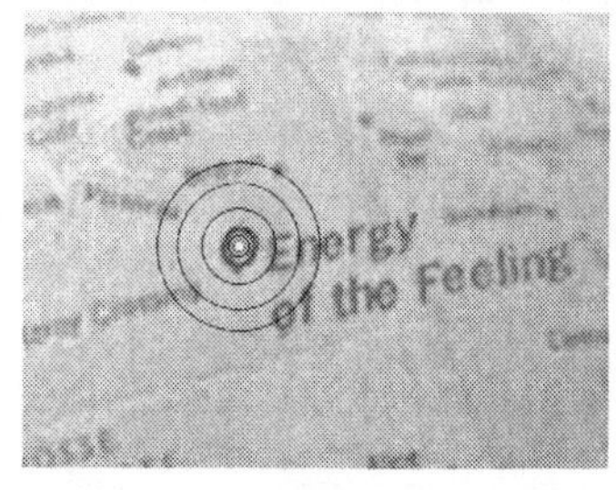

Another issue is related to the attitude toward the emotions held in your body. Due to the conditioning of *Resisting Feeling Things Fully*, we typically strive to "Make the bad feeling go away!" This is simply because we're afraid of being overwhelmed by the feeling. We've had an entire lifetime of perpetuating the childhood notion that we can't handle the feeling and are going to be overwhelmed by it.

This can cause us to try to move too quickly—to *force* the completion of experiencing the energy of the feeling. But you must understand that the CORE Technique is not about "making the feeling go away" or "getting rid of the feeling." It is about having a truly complete experience of the energy of the feelings in your body. Forcing the process will tend to cause straining and resistance, which can actually *get in the way* of allowing yourself to truly complete the experience. When the feeling is completely gone, it is gone by virtue of completing the experience not by having made it go away. This is a subtle but important difference.

It took me years to realize this simple idea, but now I understand that when there is incomplete emotional energy stored in the body, there is simply some experience our body is trying to get us to complete. The attitude of "getting rid of it" tends to cause us to stuff or repress the feeling. This ignores the body's innate intelligence, which is trying to offer us what I call "experiential wisdom." The completion of the experience of truly feeling the energy of an emotion in the body grants us the experiential wisdom that enables the body to stop needing to create that energy any more.

Remember, the CORE Technique is all about gaining the skill of completing incomplete experiences. So it is really important to shift your attitude from one of "making it go away" to one that will allow you to simply complete the experience of whatever energy you've been holding there.

Laser-like Focus

Sometimes during the process of practicing the CORE Technique, it can seem to take a long time to complete the experience of intense energy from backlogged emotions. When this happens, it is often the expression of some of the subtle influences of the Core Dynamic of *Resisting Feeling Things Fully*. If you are in the habit of moving away from where the energy of the sensation is most intense, your awareness may tend to spread out—kind of like a flashlight beam. If your awareness is more like a flashlight beam, you will tend not to complete the experience of the energy of the feeling very quickly. Although we aren't in a rush when we're doing the CORE Technique, we do want to be efficient about completing the experience.

If you feel like the focus of your awareness on the center of the feeling is too diffuse, like a wide flashlight beam lighting up a big expanse, try this simple exercise:

As you move to the center of the energy of the feeling, imagine that your awareness is a super-fine laser beam—the most precise laser beam ever invented. Allow this laser beam to guide you right into the very center—the most intense part—of the energy. This simple exercise can make a big difference in how long it takes to complete the experience. Because the CORE Technique is all about finding the most concentrated part of the energy of the feeling, it is really important to try this exercise, if necessary.

This is not to say that one couldn't resolve these experiences with a flashlight beam. But as I mentioned before, we want to be as efficient as possible. This is not, as with therapy, about spending a lot of time re-experiencing things. We want to take as much time as necessary to fully experience the energy of our old stored emotions, and then move on. When we use a laser-like focus of our awareness, it can make the difference between spending moments in the process, and spending hours or even days to complete it.

Like learning a musical instrument, you'll find that you become more effective with practice. Each time you do the technique you'll get better and better at it. After doing the CORE Technique a couple of dozen times, you'll discover to your delight that you can feel down into the energy of a feeling with laser-like precision, and the process will be completed sometimes literally in seconds.

chapter 14

Subtle Variations of the CORE Technique

Now I'll tell you about some of the different kinds of experiences you may have with the CORE Technique, and give you some of its refinements and subtleties. There is a wide range of possible experiences using the CORE Technique, and as you do it more often, you may experience some of them. We have found that it is useful to be prepared to discover your inner landscape of stored emotional energies, so that you will not resist your natural experiences or become concerned if any of these things show up.

The Eye of the Hurricane

As explained earlier, sometimes as you feel down into the energy of the sensation or feeling in the body, it will seem as if there is a vortex, a kind of hurricane's eye, right in the center of the energy. If you experience this, let your awareness be like a laser beam going right down the center of the vortex. Keep following it down until you "come out the bottom," and it will open up into the experience of Pure Awareness.

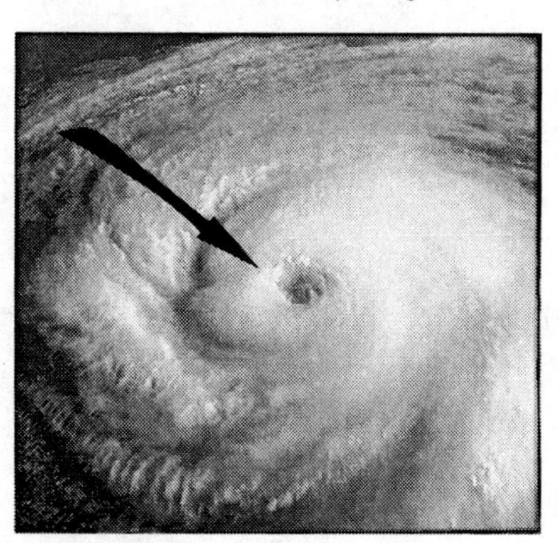

What if I feel like crying?

Sometimes you may feel the energy is just too intense, and you may feel inclined to let yourself be sucked into it or overwhelmed by it. You may feel like you are about to cry. There's nothing wrong with crying, but it may not be the most efficient way to completely resolve the energy of the incomplete emotion that is held there.

If you think about it for a moment, at what age did you learn to be overwhelmed by emotions and collapse into the overwhelming feeling and cry? Pretty young, that's for sure! Allowing yourself to collapse into crying and be overwhelmed by the energy of an emotion is a learned behavior from a time when your capacity to feel things was much smaller than it is now. You were very young and had a delicate nervous system that was easily overwhelmed. You developed the habit of crying at that time because it was all you could do.

Certainly there is some release from the emotion that happens from crying, but often there will still be residual energy there that can be triggered again by certain circumstances. Crying then becomes yet another way to avoid feeling into the core of the energy. I understand that this may seem counterintuitive. After all, we live in an age that is finally making it more acceptable to feel things and show our emotions. I certainly don't want to discourage anyone from the very natural experience of crying, when it is appropriate. But my experience has shown to achieve our true aim—resolving these incomplete experiences that are being held in the body so thoroughly and completely that they no longer are a barrier to our experiencing Pure Awareness all the time—crying can actually be a hindrance. You see, as long as you continue to avoid feeling these incomplete feelings held in the body, they act as a kind of screen between you and a natural state of inner peace. It is this "screen" that tends to keep you in a state of anxiety.

I have consistently found that instead of crying, it is usually much more helpful to take one's awareness to the center of the intensity of the incomplete emotional energy and feel down into it until the experience is complete. This will free you from any residual energy that the body is trying to get you to feel. The body is very tenacious. It will keep producing the same energy until you allow yourself to complete that experience. Once it is complete you are free of it forever.

It's like running anti-virus software on yourself. Once the virus is gone, it's gone and won't come back unless you have another traumatic experience similar to the previous one that put it there. But there is very little likelihood that this will happen, because you are much stronger now. You know how to do the CORE Technique, which will help prevent already-completed energy from ever coming back.

First of all, even if you do have another overwhelming experience that is similar to the one you completed, you have the CORE Technique that you can use to complete any new or similar incompletion you may encounter. You're already good at this, so there's no problem! More importantly, as you practice the CORE Technique over time, you will gain the skill of staying present for intense emotional experiences without being overwhelmed. You'll be able to experience emotional intensity much more easily because you will have been exercising and expanding your capacity to feel. And when you fully experience things in the moment, as they happen, your body doesn't have to store the incomplete emotional energy for later processing. Think of the freedom you'll experience!

chapter 15

Remembering to Use the CORE Technique

"Almost every time I notice a reaction to something emotional or mental, I have learned to find the area where I feel it, embrace it, and then watch and feel it dissolve. It is amazing the changes it has made in my life. I now find that the moment I feel a reaction, I do the CORE Technique, usually in seconds. Those things that used to bother me don't have a charge or much charge anymore."

—Elizabeth Witcofski, Phoenix, AZ

The most important aspect of the CORE Technique is not, as you might think, "getting it perfect." As with any new skill, like meditation or learning to play an instrument, the most important thing is simply to practice. So the most important thing about the CORE Technique is... remembering to use it! Once you have learned it and put it to use, you've upgraded your inner human software. It is as if you now have a new icon for an "inner human software" program sitting on your "inner desktop."

Just like with computer software, though, this new upgraded software isn't going to do you much good unless you double click on it and use it! In other words, don't just "learn" the techniques in this book like a subject in school. There's no exam at the end of the book! Instead of learning them, *use them.* Incorporate them into your daily life so that if you find you are caught in the grip of anxiety and fear—or for that matter, any strong emotion you experience—you don't have to stay stuck there.

The best way to remember to use this wonderful new tool is to make a *decision* that you are going to become really good at it and that you are going to use it every time you feel anxious or worried. As Anthony Robbins said in *Awaken the Giant Within*, "I believe that it's in your moments of *decision* that your destiny is shaped."[10] If you make a real decision to bring the CORE Technique into your life, you will follow through effortlessly. After you have done the CORE Technique a couple of dozen times you will have probably overcome your reticence about feeling your feelings so fully. Then the CORE Technique will simply become a normal part of your skill set, like reading silently. You won't have to try hard to remember to use it because it will have become a natural part of your life. It will be right there and you'll use it whenever the need arises.

One of your challenges will be that you are already very used to having anxiety. It's familiar to you. And you may have had it so long that it seems normal. So one tricky issue is going to be recognizing that you are in an anxious state and then remembering to do this special application of the CORE Technique to vaporize the underlying fear that is at the basis of your anxiety.

However, the good news is that you don't even need to know exactly what you're anxious about! And you don't need to know what the deeper fear at the basis of your anxious feelings is either. You might get an occasional insight into what the deeper cause of the anxiety is, but the truth is, it really doesn't matter. An intellectual understanding of the origins of your fear rarely makes that fear go away, as you may already know very well. What's needed is to vaporize the underlying fear experientially. Then the experience of the energy of the fear gets completed and the anxiety is vaporized.

10 Robbins, Anthony. Awaken the Giant Within. Free Press, New York. 1991. pp. 32-33.

All you have to do is to find somewhere you can sit quietly, close your eyes, and scan your body. First you will probably find some generalized anxiety feelings or you might have a feeling of getting panicky. As you allow yourself to feel the whole field of the anxious feeling, you will usually start to feel some tightness or ache or emptiness or some kind of feeling somewhere in your body. When you find it, use the CORE Technique to feel down into it completely until there is nothing left to feel.

When you're done, you can check to see if there's any anxiety left. You'll often find that it is gone. If it isn't, that means there's something else left to feel. Scan your body again and feel into and complete anything that your body is calling out to you to feel. If it still isn't completed, use the SEE Technique that is explained later in the book. Between the CORE and the SEE techniques, anxiety doesn't stand a chance of continuing to spoil your life!

When you have completed even one of the fears that has been causing your anxiety, you will feel a renewed sense of peace and silence inside. The anxiety will be gone because you have completed the experience of the underlying fear that you had been avoiding by staying out at the edges of the field of energy of the feeling. Once you have this experience a few times you'll be able to remember to use the CORE Technique whenever you need it.

chapter 16

EEG Validation of the CORE Technique

In January of 2007 I attended a conference on neurofeedback in Palm Springs, CA called "The Winter Brain Meeting." During the conference I had the opportunity to test a new form of EEG monitoring equipment from iCAP that allows one to see the brain wave indications of deep emotional releases that people get using the CORE Technique.

Great Life Technologies had a booth at the conference and I was mainly there to share our recent successes with debugging the underlying causes of ADD and ADHD using Human Software Engineering.[11] I gave a presentation about our work with this new approach. I also had the opportunity to give numerous demonstrations. People were fascinated, and many practitioners, heads of large clinics, and neurofeedback device manufacturers became very interested in Human Software Engineering.

I began to explain the Core Dynamics of Common Problems to a woman at the conference who was fascinated with our work and wanted to know more. As we talked, she shared that the past year had been difficult for her, and that she was feeling stressed and very anxious as a result. She was a mid-level executive at a large company, and had been considering a change of career. She had never experienced anxiety before this period, which in itself was probably contributing greatly to her anxiety. (By the way, this is a very common

11 My next book, titled Vaporize Your ADD/ADHD, will be published in Summer 2008. For more information, please visit www.VaporizeYourADD.com

situation for people who have an onset of anxiety later in life).

I helped her to identify where in her body she was holding the energy of all of this stress. It turned out to be in her solar plexus, which was very interesting. In the Eastern religious traditions, the site of the 3rd chakra is the solar plexus. It is sometimes called "The Power Chakra" and is associated with will power, vitality, and personal power. According to Eastern tradition, when people are out of balance in this chakra, they will often experience feelings of powerlessness: fear of taking risks, fear of confronting people or issues, fear of taking charge. In other words, they are stuck "dancing at the outer edges of fear," and they commonly experience what we call "anxiety."

Using one of the advanced Core Dynamics coaching techniques, I debugged her inner human software for the Core Dynamic *Resisting Feeling Things Fully*, and I explained the nature of the kind of pre-verbal, pre-cognitive conditioning that produces our inner resistance to self-healing this kind of stress. I was just starting to teach her the CORE Technique and thought to ask her if she'd like to do this while using the new iCAP EEG monitoring device. This would allow us to see the effect of the technique on her brain waves. She said she would like to try this, so we went to the iCAP booth that was right next to the Great Life Technologies booth and asked if we could use it. The iCAP folks were very enthusiastic about it, especially since it was so simple to put on the headband, turn the unit on and start the software on the laptop.

As I guided her into the CORE of the feeling I got to watch what was happening with the EEG on the monitor. With the iCAP system, a drop in the indicator line means that there is a release of stress and/or emotional energy occurring. At a certain point, about three and a half minutes into the session, and after a short instruction about allowing herself to go right into the center of the most intense part of the energy of the feeling, there was a dramatic drop in the EEG indicator line.

Right at that moment, one of the founders of the iCAP company who was sitting nearby happened to look over. When he saw what was happening on the monitor at that moment, his eyes widened and his jaw dropped open! He waited for a few moments, because he could see that she was in the middle of a resolving something huge from the indicator on the monitor. Then he said quietly (but with a strong enthusiasm in his voice), "Wow, your stuff really works! Getting below 300 is really extraordinary!" (In fact, the reading from the EEG had gone down into the 270's range during that big drop.)

Here's what it looked like on the screen (with my notations added). There are two overlapping traces, one for the signal from the first 2 ½ minutes of the exercise and one that shows the activity of the second 2 ½ minutes. She was starting to get the hang of it toward the end of the first 2 ½ minutes, then even more during the first 30 seconds of the second 2 ½ minutes as you can see from the traces. At about 45 seconds into the section 2 ½ minutes, she completely let go of the big knot of stress that she had been holding onto. Later she said that it was the cumulative stress of the entire past year and that she felt transformed during these few minutes.

EEG Brain Scan

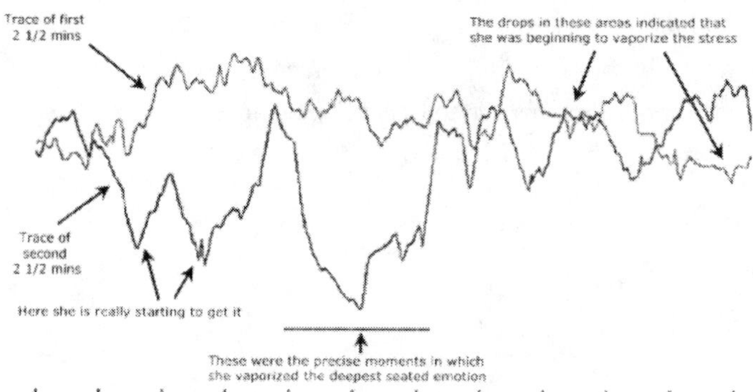

It was great to meet the people from the iCAP company and learn about their new EEG technology. It's a unique new form of EEG monitoring that is specifically designed to pick up and display brain wave patterns that indicate deep emotional releases. Best of all, its very user friendly—it's completely wireless, and it doesn't even require moisture for the sensor that picks up the brain waves (and at about $1,250 it is priced for the general public!). The small sensing unit is mounted in a simple headband and sends a wireless signal to a small USB receiving device that brings the data into a very simple interface on your computer. The software allows you to witness in real time the direct effect of doing techniques that release emotions and create a deep state of relaxation. And in addition to monitoring the emotional releases that occur in the moment, it can track your progress in cleaning out your emotional baggage over time. We are happy to endorse this great new product and make it available at our website.

If you are intrigued by the ways technology can contribute to the understanding of human conditioning (I know I am!), you may enjoy reading about the iCAP EEG and other incredible technological advances that have been made recently. In addition to pioneering the field of Human Software Engineering, my company, Great Life Technologies, has helped to develop and make available some of the most cutting edge equipment available anywhere in the field of human development. Visit us at **www.VaporizeYourAnxiety.com/technology.html** to read some fascinating articles on this topic.

chapter 17

Beyond Anxiety: How the CORE Technique Can Change Your Life

First and foremost, using the CORE Technique will liberate you from being the victim of anxiety. But the Vaporize Your Anxiety Techniques are about much more than stopping anxiety. They're about becoming someone who is more and more grounded in the experience of Pure Awareness, the essential nature of what you are. They're about becoming someone who is emotionally competent and emotionally mature. Believe it or not, vaporizing your anxiety is actually one of the smallest rewards that you will be getting from learning and using the exercises in this book and becoming competent at using these techniques.

As you use the CORE technique more and more, you'll find that you're in the process of dismantling many of the strategies you use to avoid being overwhelmed. This will allow you to start being more true to yourself, to start trusting and consistently acting on your intuition, and to become much less judgmental of others and yourself. Those around you will instantly recognize this and notice that you have an energy and vitality in your life that wasn't there before.

In Malcolm Gladwell's wonderful book *Blink*, he describes the amazing things that happen when people act on their intuition. Multi-million dollar pieces already purchased by major museums have been exposed as frauds. Lives of heart-attack victims have been saved by ER doctors who trusted their own intuition more than the machinery designed to diagnose their patients. Time and time again, major cultural shifts have been the result of people's split-second decisions that were based on two things: strong intuition and immediate action with *no second-guessing.*

Another thing that will happen to you as you practice the CORE Technique regularly is that you will gain the capacity to be fully present for everything that comes your way in life. One of the primary difficulties in intimate relationships is that one or both people have a hard time actually "being there" with the other person. They are distracted by their own concerns and fears. As a result, their partners can end up feeling lonely and left out. Working through your incomplete emotional experiences will allow you to really show up for your life and the people in it, and you'll be appreciated for it in ways you may never have imagined.

What all of these things have in common is that they require the ability to feel fully. When you develop that skill, you'll find that you can stack the cards in your favor by working on resolving your backlog of emotional pain and fear before stressful events even have a chance to trigger it. These are archived fears that can cause you to feel anxious in the future if left un-vaporized. The good news is that your database of fear and emotional pain is finite. It does not go on forever. That means that every time you complete one of these unresolved experiences, it is truly vaporized—that one isn't coming back. You are becoming more and more free of the underlying causes of anxiety. Soon it will be a thing of the past.

And remember, your ability and effectiveness in using the CORE Technique will get better and better with practice. Your body will be getting more and more free of fear and emotional pain. This builds a positively reinforcing cycle in which, each time you resolve a fearful or painful emotion, you gain even more access to your true self, which in turn encourages you to work on resolving more and more of that backlog of emotional pain. You will experience a continuous and cumulative upgrading of your capacity to feel and be present. As you resolve each held fear, emotional pain, stress or trauma, it opens your awareness more and more to *Pure Awareness*, that state of blissful purity where you can finally experience what and who you truly are.

chapter 18

The GAP Technique: Easily Accessing Inner Peace

As someone who suffers from anxiety, it may be encouraging for you to hear that I have developed a technique that will allow you to easily access inner peace. I call it the GAP technique. GAP stands for "Greater Awareness Place," and the GAP Technique is a way to quickly and directly experience a state of inner peace in a matter of moments. It's a very simple technique that anyone can do. In this section of the book we'll go into the description of the GAP Technique in a detail and also explain when to use it, how to handle thoughts that come up during it, and cover some special applications of the GAP Technique.

Recent scientific research in neuroscience confirms that there are periods of inactivity in the brain that correspond to the gaps between thoughts. And if you pay attention to your thoughts for a while, just observing them as they come and go, you'll notice that they are not continuous. One thought begins, has a particular duration, and then ends before the next thought begins. It is the gap between the thoughts that we are interested in noticing here, because it is in those gaps that Pure Awareness resides.

Practicing the GAP Technique can rapidly bring you the clear, direct experience of Pure Awareness, which in turn brings a profound sense of inner peace, centeredness, relaxation and expansion of awareness. As you gradually increase your familiarity with Pure Awareness, you begin to sense a shift in your sense of who you are. You move from thinking of yourself as an anxious, isolated individual to experiencing yourself as the totality of Pure Awareness, connected to all others on Earth and alive to the connectedness that is our true state of being.

This would be a good time to take a few minutes to experience Pure Awareness again. One of the simplest and most effective ways to do this is to listen to an audio recording of me guiding someone through it. You can just follow along and do the technique yourself by simply listening and following the simple instructions. I've made a recording available for you at **http://www.vaporizeyouranxiety.com/resources.html**

If you don't have Internet access, you can have someone read you the script below. Because the GAP Technique takes the mind inward to a place of deep quietness, this will work better than going back and forth between reading and then closing your eyes again to do the next step of the technique. Opening your eyes in the middle of this process, especially several times, will tend to disrupt the process of going inward.

Exercise: Experience the gap between thoughts

The purpose of this exercise is to shift the attention from an outward direction to an inward direction so that it is possible to experience the essential nature of awareness itself.

Have someone read you the following script:

(Instructions for the person reading: *If you were the reader for the CORE Technique earlier in the book, this will be familiar to you. The approach is the same: read the* "**bold sections in quotation marks**" *out loud and read the italicized sections silently to yourself.)*

"Please sit comfortably and close your eyes."

Wait for about half a minute.

"Notice that with your eyes closed you experience several kinds of things. You hear my voice, you may notice feeling your body sitting in the chair, you may notice other noises or sensations, and you will notice that there are thoughts coming to you."

Pause

"Notice that the thoughts are like speaking; they don't come in one long run-on sentence. There are pauses or gaps, sometimes very brief, in between the thoughts."

Pause

"So just allow yourself to notice the gaps in between the thoughts."

Now wait for about half a minute.

"Notice that the gaps between thoughts are truly empty. There is nothing there. It's just Pure Awareness without the awareness of anything else. It is lively but there is no object of experience."

Pause

"Another way to directly experience this nothingness of Pure Awareness is to simply notice that the thoughts you experience in your mind are occurring in a background of silence. Some people find it easier to just shift their attention from noticing the activity of the thoughts to noticing the silent background in which the thoughts are occurring.

Pause

"As you notice the silent background in which the thoughts are occurring, you will notice that you can be aware of it even while the thoughts are coming and going. Allow yourself to simply favor noticing that silent background. Immerse yourself in that silence."

Wait about one minute

"If you find that you have become absorbed in thinking, at the moment when you notice this, simply bring your attention back to the silent background in which the thoughts are occuring."

Wait one to two minutes here.

"Okay. When you're ready, open your eyes."

When the person has opened their eyes please ask them the following:

What did you experience?

What was it like?

What are the attributes of that background of silence?

You may get responses such as: "It's quiet." "It's peaceful." "It's expansive." "It's pleasant." "It's relaxing." "It's very nice."

This is the end of the script for guiding someone through the GAP Technique.

From here, you can begin reading the book again yourself.

Take a moment to jot down the answers to the following three questions. If you'd like to add anything, feel free. Don't try to force it or make it more than it was. Just let your answers flow naturally.

What did you experience?

What are the attributes of that background of silence?

What was it like, compared to your experiences of anxiety?

Now that you have experienced your own *Pure Awareness*, it is easy to notice that it is always there, lively in the background, even with your eyes open and with the activity of experiencing the objects of the senses. Can you still feel the presence of *Pure Awareness*? Is there anything lacking in that experience? Is there any sense of anxiety or fear while you're in the place of *Pure Awareness*? Is there anything that you could not do from this place? If you're like most people, tasting *Pure Awareness* is like simultaneously becoming aware of true peace and true power.

If you aren't sure whether you had a clear experience of *Pure Awareness* or not, don't worry. This is common. After all, remember that every experience you have is an experience of some THING, some object of perception. Our lives are so focused in an outward direction that we tend not to realize or remember that this silent *Pure Awareness* is the essence of what we are. Because there is literally "no-thing" there,

Pure Awareness can seem very abstract and so completely unlike our other experiences, that when you first experience it you may not be sure that you did.

After all, our only database of experiences prior to a few moments ago was of the experience of things as things. So if you aren't sure if you experienced it, just try going through the exercise again. Remember, you're not trying to experience something that's an object. It's just the silent witness of your experiences, just your awareness itself, that with which you experience everything else.

Now that you have directly experienced *Pure Awareness*, you may see what I mean by how simple and easy it is to have this experience. This is because there is nowhere to go, there is nothing to do. It is just a matter of noticing the background of silence in which your thoughts and perceptions are occurring. That's it. It is simply your own awareness being aware of itself!

More on the GAP Technique

Now that you have experienced *Pure Awareness* by accessing it using the GAP Technique, I'd like to give you a little bit more insight about the technique, and how to get the most out of it.

Although you now know the basics of how to do the GAP Technique, there are some subtleties that will be helpful to know about. You may have noticed that there are two ways to access *Pure Awareness* during the GAP Technique, which are detailed below. Both of them are easier to achieve with your eyes closed. In both cases, a good way to start is to simply allow yourself to become aware of your thoughts as they occur in your mind.

Notice The Gaps Between Thoughts

The first way to access *Pure Awareness* is simply notice that that there are gaps or pauses in between your thoughts. This may sound too simple at first, but it can be surprisingly effective. In fact, there is now scientific evidence showing periods of inactivity between thoughts that amount to "gaps." If it seems like there aren't any gaps at all, don't despair! This is normal, especially when your mind is racing or when you're very anxious, emotionally upset, or disturbed. If this is the case, what is usually needed is a shift to the CORE Technique to complete the incomplete experience that is currently dominating your inner experience. Once you do this and it's complete, you will have a more settled state of being and you'll be able to notice the gaps in between your thoughts.

Find the Background of Silence

The second way to access *Pure Awareness* is to notice that your thoughts are occurring against a *background of silence.* Normally we don't pay any attention to this background of silence, of course. When we're listening to music in our living room, we don't pay attention to the fact (or even realize) that this music is actually playing against a background of silence, and that the silent background is what makes hearing the music possible in the first place. Likewise, when we go to the movies we become absorbed in the images that are projected onto the screen, without paying attention to or even remembering the blank white screen that allows the images to be seen. Even though the white screen is there we don't see it when it is covered up by the images and activity of the movie.

Similarly, the background of silence against which our thoughts occur is usually "covered up" by the "volume" of the sounds or images of our thoughts. Our thoughts are active, have meaning, sometimes have emotions associated with them, and they are certainly more engaging at the level of "content" than the background of silence in which they are occurring. So thoughts tend to attract our attention more than the silence does. Like the white screen at the movie theater, we usually don't even know it is there until we actually experience it—as you just have.

It is an amazing thing: if we want to experience our essential nature—our very own *Pure Awareness*—it's a simple matter of "looking off to the side" of the thoughts and noticing that these thoughts are occurring in a background of silence.

Interestingly enough, this can be done even when the mind is racing with lots of thoughts that don't seem to have any gaps between them. This may be why some people prefer the "looking off to the side of the thoughts" approach over noticing the gaps, but either one will give you access to the delightful, perhaps even divine experience of *Pure Awareness*.

Thoughts, Thoughts and More Thoughts—What Can I Do?

A common feature of people who are anxious is that they feel bombarded by thoughts. While practicing the GAP Technique you may become concerned that you're getting absorbed in thinking, and that this seems to be getting in the way of the experience of *Pure Awareness*. It's important to understand the role of thoughts during the GAP Technique and to know how to handle them.

The answer is that there is nothing to handle. I'm not making a bad joke—having thoughts occur is really *not* a barrier to experiencing Pure Awareness. It is perfectly possible to experience *Pure Awareness* and have thoughts occurring at the same time. It's just a matter of noticing what you favor with your attention. It's certainly true that we are deeply habituated to noticing our thoughts. I would go so far as

to say that just about everyone seems to be addicted to thinking. In fact, my experience is that many people actually use being absorbed in thinking as a "drug of choice" to avoid feeling things.

But this doesn't mean you can't experience the background of silence even while thoughts are occurring. You can simply choose to shift your attention from noticing thoughts to noticing the background of silence. You can allow yourself to really immerse your attention in that silent background. When you do this it is quite easy to simply allow yourself to shift your attention away from the thoughts and more toward noticing the background of silence. Just as you can read a book with birds chirping outside or with the hum of traffic on the freeway a few blocks way, you have the ability to direct your awareness to favor noticing one thing more than something else. It's just that we are so deeply conditioned to only notice our thoughts that most of us don't even realize there is a silent background in which the thoughts are occurring.

As you practice noticing *Pure Awareness*—that background of silence in which the thoughts occur—you may begin to have some extended periods of very clear experiences of *Pure Awareness*. Sometimes there won't seem to be any thoughts at all. The thoughts may seem to fade so deeply into the background that you hardly notice them. When this happens it can be a very powerful and satisfying experience. You will feel deeply refreshed and fully alive while also feeling deeply rested and relaxed.

As you practice the GAP Technique for longer periods of time, say 10 to 20 minutes, you may also have experiences of becoming absorbed in thinking for what seem to be long periods of many minutes. Sometimes when this happens people think that they are doing the GAP Technique incorrectly or that something is wrong with what they are doing. Nothing could be further from the truth.

When you become lost to thoughts during the GAP Technique this is actually because the technique is working beautifully!

This may seem like a strange proposition. How could it be working if the idea is to experience the GAP and not the thoughts? There is a very special answer to this question that will allow you to take a whole new attitude towards the thoughts that occur while you are doing the GAP Technique. Here it is:

When you shift your attention to noticing the background of silence in which the thoughts are occurring, you are favoring noticing a state within you that's much less active than the active mind—the one that's usually busy thinking thoughts. As you shift your attention to noticing *Pure Awareness* you will sometimes notice that you feel very relaxed. This is because you are naturally giving less energy to the mental activity of thinking.

We tend to think of our body and mind as separate things, but the truth is that they are both parts of one wholeness—*who we are*. When we begin to notice the silent background of *Pure Awareness* and naturally experience less mental activity, an amazing thing happens: our mind settles down. And as our mind settles down, our body naturally settles down as well. This allows us to feel deeply relaxed. During this relaxation it is also natural for the body to begin to release any stresses or strains that may have accumulated.

When stresses and strains begin to be released in the body, this creates movement or activity in the body. This activity naturally creates new movement and activity in our mind because as we've already noted, the mind and body are intimately connected. This means that when you become absorbed in thoughts while practicing the GAP Technique, it is actually a very positive by-product of the phenomenon of releasing stresses and strains. I've also had people fall asleep during the GAP Technique. This might seem like a very different kind of response from becoming absorbed in thoughts, but it is actually the same thing in a different wrapper. It's just the body releasing accumulated fatigue, so you fall asleep. It's all quite natural. When you do the GAP Technique, your body will take the opportunity to give itself what it needs, whether that means releasing stress, fatigue or other energies. This is just a wonderful example of the naturally integrated functioning of the mind and body.

So if you have lots of thoughts during a particular session of the GAP Technique, it actually means that you have successfully accessed the GAP and settled the mind down, even if it's only for a short time. It means that the body is releasing some stresses and strains. This in turn is creating the activity of thinking in a strong enough way that your mind becomes quite occupied with this activity. This is experienced as thoughts in the mind. It's not from doing it wrong. On the contrary, it is from doing the technique correctly!

So don't have the attitude that thoughts shouldn't be there. It's natural for them to be there. It is also natural for you to shift from noticing *Pure Awareness* to noticing the thoughts. When this happens, here's what you can do about it:

When you notice that you have been absorbed in thinking, don't bother to chastise yourself. Actually, something good has just happened—you've released some stress. When the body has released enough stress that you become aware that you've been thinking, now it is time to go back into the GAP and experience *Pure Awareness* again. When you become aware that you were thinking, gently shift your attention back to noticing the background of silence in which the thoughts are occurring.

Simply allow for the naturalness of both thinking and noticing *Pure Awareness* in the background of silence. There is a natural shifting back and forth between noticing Pure Awareness and being absorbed in thinking. The idea, after all, is to cultivate a clean inner landscape using the CORE Technique and to become completely familiar with Pure Awareness using the GAP Technique. Eventually, you will no longer lose the experience of *Pure Awareness*, and it won't be overshadowed by thoughts or by anything else.

When you develop this state of being, you come to experience the presence of *Pure* Awareness all the time, 24/7/365—it never goes away. And that's what we're after. When you get to this state (which you can actually reach quite quickly, simply by regularly using the *Pure Awareness Techniques*), you will be able to maintain the experience of *Pure Awareness* not only while you're having thoughts, but even while you're having intense experiences of pleasure or pain. In this state you're never lost to your experiences, and you experience a shift from being an individual to being *Pure Awareness*, which is the true reality of what you really are. In this state anxiety doesn't exist. It permanently becomes a non-issue and you are never anxious ever again.

When to Use the GAP Technique

You can use the GAP Technique whenever you like, whenever you want to experience *Pure Awareness.* Some people like to make a regular practice of the GAP Technique and use it as a form of meditation that they do once or twice a day, typically in the morning and evening. Another time you may find the GAP Technique particularly beneficial is before doing something where you would benefit from being in a place of wholeness, such as giving a presentation or having an important meeting. Or you might just like to take a moment out of your busy, stressful day to experience *Pure Awareness.* It's a rejuvenating experience! As you practice it, you will cultivate the presence of *Pure Awareness* in your life.

At a recent meeting that I was holding with a team of people who are working on bringing Core Dynamics coaching and training programs into the corporate workplace we started the team meeting by having everyone go into the GAP. What followed was the most amazing meeting experience most of us had ever had. The meeting flowed beautifully and the creativity was extraordinary. We finished the meeting an hour and a half ahead of schedule with surprising outcomes that were far better than what we had anticipated from our original agenda. After that, we made the decision to start all of our meetings this way!

Core Dynamics Coaches who work with top-level executives in different countries around the world are using the GAP technique to start their training sessions with these executives. The execs are amazed at the new levels of cooperation, communication and progress that they are making.

Although incorporating the GAP Technique into your life and making it a regular practice is highly recommended, don't overdo it. Sitting around doing the GAP Technique for hours at a time may not be the best plan for integrating the state of *Pure Awareness* into your life. What is optimal is to toggle back and forth between becoming familiar with *Pure Awareness* by doing the GAP Technique for short periods of time and then engaging in your daily activities. Balance is the key, and introducing the GAP Technique into your daily routine starts you on a path of integrating Pure Awareness into your life experience. The value of doing this is enormous.

The GAP Technique is also very useful during Core Dynamics Coaching sessions whenever someone has become overly identified with particular things, people or events in their life. People tend to become identified and attached to their possessions, the people and relationships in their life, their thoughts and ideas, their emotions, expectations, reactions, stories and self-definitions. It is in the nature of human conditioning to become identified with both our inner and outer experiences and lose the sense of connection to our own essential nature—*Pure Awareness.*

During Core Dynamics Coaching sessions the Core Dynamics Coach uses the GAP technique to gently guide the client back to the experience of *Pure Awareness* when they sense a need for the person to experience the essence of who they really are. It is a great experiential antidote when you have slipped into getting the sense of who you are from anything other than *Pure Awareness.* This quickly re-establishes the inner sense of being grounded in one's Self. Many forms of attachment, struggle, and suffering just melt away and are recognized for the illusions that they are. The problems that they have caused tend to vanish in kind. The GAP Exercise is a simple and quick way to bring someone out of all of the Core Dynamics in the categories that we call *Looking for Yourself Where You Are Not* and *Trying to Force an Outcome.*

chapter 19

Sanyama and the GPS Technique

My dear friend and colleague Michael Stratford, who is the Director of the Core Dynamics Coach Training Program for Great Life Technologies, and who co-teaches this program with me, came up with a wonderful use of the GAP Technique that he calls "GPS." He had learned the GAP Technique and was practicing it regularly in order to cultivate a greater experiential familiarity with *Pure Awareness.*

On New Year's Day, 2007 he was thinking about what was coming in the year ahead, and experiencing some uncertainty. While doing the GAP technique that morning, he had the idea to go into Pure Awareness and just ask a question. What, if anything, should he do to support bringing about the things he envisioned happening in the year ahead? He just relaxed into *Pure Awareness* and listened, and some surprising answers came to him that he never would have thought of otherwise. Those answers gave him an entirely new direction for his business and coaching career. He suddenly got a level of clarity that allowed him to end his involvement with a coaching school he'd been working with for a long time, and instead focus his time and energy in new directions.

He was quite amazed by the experience, and immediately began using it with his clients. Once Michael has guided someone into *Pure Awareness* using the GAP Technique, he suggests that they simply ask any important question they'd like to have some guidance about, and encourages them to wait and see what happens. When he used this technique with his clients, he found that they would typically get some kind of "knowing" or even very clear thoughts or ideas coming to them that they had never even considered before. On one hand, they might discover that there is nothing at all to do; on the other hand, they might receive guidance about taking specific actions to bring about a particular outcome.

When Michael first told me about this technique, he said, "Dropping a question into *Pure Awareness* is like putting a destination into a GPS (Global Positioning System) device in a car. All of a sudden the path to where you want to go becomes perfectly clear." Based on this analogy, we decided to call this technique GPS, for "Gentle Provocation System."

This variation on the GAP Technique was a true revelation for me, because the process is very similar to an ancient technique described by Yogi Patanjali, an Indian sage who is thought by some to be the father of the entire field of Yoga. Patanjali described a technique called *Sanyama,* a Sanskrit word that refers to a kind of meditative awareness in which you reach a state of "luminous concentration." The outcome of this practice is the development of *Sidhis,* which translates as "perfections."

The idea is that when you drop an intention or question into Pure Awareness, it activates the laws of nature—the full power of the infinite potential that is latent in Pure Awareness. Practicing Sanyama is a powerful way to bring yourself into alignment with these laws of nature. In Sanyama, one does not command the laws of nature, but learns how to become one with them. Incredibly enough, Michael seems to have independently rediscovered some of Patanjali's insights.

Another interesting use of GPS (or the "Sanyama use of the GAP Technique") is to access any remaining energy of an incompletion. What you do is simply ask to become aware of any remaining energy of any incompletion that you might be holding onto. In this case, you're asking not for ideas or insights, but simply to be made more aware of any incomplete energy that you might still be inadvertently holding in your body.

A recent example of this comes from my experience with a client who had a very subtle fear of being vulnerable that, without being aware of it, was in fact holding him back from being even more fully successful in his life. He was teaching a course and he was finding that the students weren't responding and participating as much as he would like during each session. He was already quite familiar with the Core Dynamics, so rather than blaming the students, he took this as a cue that perhaps there was some subtle way he might be contributing to or even creating the problem with participation.

As he was sharing this experience with me we were able to identify that he had a subtle inner fear of being vulnerable or exposed and we realized that this fear was being "mirrored" to him by his students. I suggested that he go into the GAP and then make a request to be shown any remaining energy of the fear of being vulnerable. I instructed him to notice the energy that came up in his body and then to shift to the CORE Technique when he became aware of where it was being held.

I explained to him that as the energy dissolved he would either notice that it was gone, or that he might become absorbed in thinking thoughts about something else. He did this, and after a time reported that he had indeed become absorbed in thinking. When he became aware of this, he then went back into *Pure Awareness* using the GAP technique and again made the request to be shown any remaining energy related to the fear of vulnerability. After several iterations of this process, he again asked to be shown any remaining energy of the fear of being vulnerable, and this time nothing presented itself. It was just quiet and peaceful inside.

He then had the realization that he could now be fully present and self-expressed under any circumstances and felt completely free of any fear of vulnerability. The release of this deeply held but hidden fear was profound for him. When it was gone, he just laughed and laughed for several minutes because it was such a huge relief to be free of something that he hadn't even known he had been holding onto his whole life!

The key is to do this technique repeatedly until the point that when you ask to be shown any remaining energy of the emotion you get... nothing. Just to be sure you can make the request again. If you get nothing again, you are really complete with it!

GPS is a great way to make sure you have really felt every aspect of any previously incomplete emotional experience. It is also a great way to get access to incompletions that you can't name or describe with words. It is a subtle and powerful addition to the *Pure Awareness* Techniques.

chapter 20

The SEE Technique: Getting Past the Gatekeeper

Sometimes the energy of the feeling you're holding inside doesn't seem to get completed—no matter how much you use the CORE Technique and feel into the heart of it.

Why does this sometimes happen and what can we do about it?

Some emotions have been with us so long that they feel like they are a part of who we are. They aren't of course, but these feelings can be so compelling that when we attempt to feel into an emotion and complete it, there is another part of us that's afraid. Afraid, that is, that if we complete the experience, we will no longer know who we are. We shouldn't underestimate the incredible power a fear like that can have over our lives. Many people ask, "Who will I be if that feeling I've been holding onto for all these years really does go away?"

If we could articulate it we might say to ourselves

"If I complete the experience of this emotion, then part of me won't be there. I'll lose a part of myself and that's really scary. I don't like having this emotion—but then again at least it's familiar. If it's gone I won't know who I am any more."

When the energy won't resolve using the CORE Technique, no matter how much we try, we call the thing that is keeping us from resolving it a "Gatekeeper." It's like having an armored guard standing in front of the door. You just can't get in. Gatekeepers are usually the energy of the fear of letting go—in this case, letting go of something that has felt like a part of you for so long that you won't know who you are if it's gone. In the Core Dynamics model, our set of insights into the nature of pre-verbal conditioning, we call this the Core Dynamic of Resisting Change.

When we run into a Gatekeeper, the CORE Technique won't feel like it is working. But there is a way to get to Pure Awareness through a "side door" called the SEE Technique, which is a variation of the GAP Technique. SEE stands for Side Entrance Expansion. Rather than going into the CORE of the energy of the feeling, this approach does the opposite. It takes your attention out to the edges of the feeling. But instead of staying stuck in the outer edges of the feeling, you'll take your awareness just a little bit further. When you do this you'll access Pure Awareness—the silent background in which the experience of the emotion is occurring.

I was recently giving a demonstration of this technique to a woman who said that she was stuck in an ongoing state of anxiety. She had been reading my book, *Pure Awareness—Five Simple Techniques for Experiencing Your Essential Nature* and she had already been using the CORE Technique regularly. But the underlying fear simply wasn't going away. As we began to talk about her experience, she very quickly got in touch with the fear that was creating her anxious feelings. She told me that the energy of the fear was so huge that it was all consuming. She was lost to it. The fear had her in its grip.

I asked her to take her awareness out to the outer edges of the fear, which she did. I then asked her to go even a *little bit* further and notice that out beyond the outer edges of the field of energy of the fear there was quietness. This quietness is the silent background in which the experience of the fear was occurring. As she started to experience it I told her to simply favor noticing the silent background instead of continuing to be absorbed in the fear.

"Notice how vast that background of silence is," I said. "Notice that this vastness of the silent background is much bigger than the field of energy of the fear." She acknowledged this and said she could feel its vastness. I then invited her to immerse herself in the silent background. As she did this, she reported that the energy of the fear had begun to subside. It was vaporizing. Within a few minutes the fear was completely gone and when I checked in to see if there was any anxiety left she said, "What anxiety!?"

You see, the truth is that all our experiences are occurring in that background of silence, or *Pure Awareness.* And that background of silence is so vast, so unlimited, that anything you experience will be smaller than it. So if you take your awareness out past the outer edges of the field of the energy of the feeling, you'll be able to access the background of silence against which even intense emotions such as this are being experienced. If the silent background of Pure Awareness were not bigger than your experiences, then these experiences would simply overwhelm it and you would be unconscious. So as long as you are conscious you can access the background of silence, even during intense experiences.

When we're stuck inside the experience of the emotion, our true awareness has in a sense *collapsed.* We have become so identified with the emotion that it feels like we have actually *become* that emotion. It's all consuming. But once we access *Pure Awareness* using the SEE variation of the GAP Technique, whatever was causing us to be so absorbed in the emotion, so completely in its grip, softens and begins to let go.

In those moments when you're caught in the grip of an emotion, it seems as if any other sense of yourself you might once have had gets completely overshadowed by the intensity of the experience of the emotion. If you've been having these kinds of experiences over a long period of time, it's no wonder that it feels like the emotion is a part of your sense of Self. No wonder you have a hard time letting it go!

But with the SEE Technique, as you begin to experience *Pure Awareness* in the background of silence against which the intense emotion is occurring, you'll start to regain the experience of your essential nature. And there, you'll be presented with the comforting feeling of having come home to a totally safe place that is peaceful and nurturing. This is because the background of silence that is your own Pure Awareness is a field of lively pure potential that in itself isn't a "thing." It is that with which you experience everything. It is your very aliveness. And because it is limitless and easily accessible, you can always get to it out beyond the outer edges of any experience.

How to Practice the SEE Technique

The SEE Technique is very effective for awakening your awareness if it has collapsed inside an emotional reaction—especially when the reaction is triggered by an unmet expectation. It is also very useful when the CORE Technique doesn't seem to be working to complete the emotion. What follows is a "guided tour" of the SEE Technique, with all the information you need to go through the technique yourself. You may find that, as with the CORE Technique, it is easier to go through the SEE Technique with a guide. This section has been set up like the section on the CORE Technique, so that someone can easily read what is printed below and guide you through the technique.

"Sit comfortably with your eyes closed."

"Notice that the emotion you're experiencing has a field of energy to it. (If it didn't have any energy you wouldn't be able to feel it.) Sometimes the field of energy of the emotion feels like it's inside your body. Other times it may feel like the energy of the emotion extends outside your body or that it is enveloping you—like you're inside a bubble or cloud of emotional energy. But in either case, you tend to feel like you're inside the experience of the emotion."

"Now, notice that the field of energy of the emotion has an outer limit. It may extend beyond your physical body, but it doesn't go on forever. There is an outer edge of the energy field which might be very well defined or kind of vague."

Pause

"Notice where the outer edge of the energy field of the emotion is, and that there is nothing else beyond it."

Pause

"Now take your awareness a little further beyond the outer edge of the emotion and notice that there is some quietness there."

Pause

"Now go even further from the outer edge of the emotion more deeply into the quietness that surrounds the field of its energy."

Pause

"Notice that this quietness surrounding the energy of the emotion is much bigger than the emotion itself."

Pause

"Now notice that this quietness is actually a background of silence in which the emotion is occurring."

Pause

"Notice that this background of silence doesn't have any limits. Take a little time to simply notice and enjoy how enormous and vast this background of silence is."

Pause

"Now notice what is happening to the field of the energy of the emotion that we started with.

It is probably shrinking or fading away."

Pause

"Notice that the emotion was being caused by a reaction to something you expected to happen—but that in the end didn't actually happen."

Pause

"Also notice that the expectation was not something real, but only a story you made up. Notice how unimportant it seems now."

Pause

"Notice how, from the perspective of the vastness of the silent background, your story, the expectation and the reaction don't seem to have as much grip on you as they did before."

Pause

"Now just allow yourself to be in the vastness of the silent background, until there is nothing left of the energy of the emotion or the expectation. It wasn't real to begin with. Enjoy the profound feeling of freedom that comes from knowing that your expectation and reaction were just illusions."

Conclusion

Over the years, it has become clear to me that the problems people have in their lives are almost always caused by the loss of the experience of Wholeness—the loss of the connection to their essential nature, or *Pure Awareness*. The real answer to moving beyond your problems is to regain that experience, which is your birthright. And that's just what the techniques in this book are about. They are about rediscovering and reclaiming the unique human experience of Wholeness.

Now that you have learned, experienced and practiced the Vaporize Your Anxiety techniques, you may already have made major progress toward resolving your anxiety. As I've said throughout the book, to successfully Vaporize Your Anxiety you must actually do the techniques. The thing to keep in mind is that most people need to practice them for some time in order to thoroughly clean house and cleanse their inner emotional landscape of all of the emotional baggage they've accumulated throughout their lives. So don't stop before you've practiced enough, because what you'll find is that when you've truly completed the experience of all of those incomplete emotional energies and extracted yourself from your absorption in reactions to expectations, you simply won't feel anxious anymore.

If you've tried these techniques on your own and you aren't making the progress you'd like to, or if you simply feel blocked, don't worry! This is quite common. It's generally because your conditioning is getting the best of you. Think about it: in order to do these techniques successfully, you essentially have to do things that are the exact opposite of what you have been deeply conditioned to do, since infancy! This is why working with a Core Dynamics Coach can be so powerful. As you're gently guided through and beyond your conditioning by a Master Coach, you'll find that you eventually reach a place where it no longer has the power to control your life.

My experience has been that some sessions with a qualified Core Dynamics Coach will often resolve a person's anxiety for good. Then once you get the hang of doing these techniques you'll start to become self-sufficient and you'll be able to do the techniques on your own, if and when you need to. And if you ever feel like you're slipping back into a pattern of anxious feelings (which would be rare) you'll have the skill and experience to resolve it yourself in almost every case.

My wish for you is that you'll learn and use the techniques in this book to grant yourself a life completely free from anxiety and free of problems; a life of freedom, peace, and true enjoyment of all the richness that your life has to offer. That's what's possible when you really integrate these techniques into your life.

From the forward to Tom's book *Pure Awareness*

Jack Canfield, Co-author, *Chicken Soup for the Soul*® series and *The Success Principles*™*: How to Get from Where You Are to Where You Want to Be.*

I was giving a seminar for a local business at a hotel in Fairfield, Iowa in December 1993. Tom Stone happened to be having lunch that day at the hotel restaurant. I was having lunch there as well with some of the participants from the seminar. A friend of Tom's was among them, and as she and I were walking back from the salad bar, she stopped and introduced me to Tom.

"They tell me you're a walking miracle," I said. Less than five weeks earlier, Tom had been shot in the chest at close range with a .44 caliber handgun by a stranger and survived. Now he was up and walking around, even having lunch out. Tom's friend had already mentioned this incident to me. She had also told me a little bit about Tom's expert use of kinesiology, also known as muscle testing. The three of us chatted and arranged for Tom to come to the hotel that evening and give me a private session.

That evening when Tom arrived, I only had an hour before I was going to be picked up and taken to another appointment. But Tom quickly identified what was going on.

"What's bothering you?" he asked.

"I want to affect the lives of a larger number of people," I replied. "I want to help more people and have a bigger impact. I feel like I'm on a plateau—that I'm settling for less than I really want. We then spent some time discussing what it was that I wanted and crafting a positive intention statement."

Tom explained that there were "inner conflicts" that were blocking me from manifesting this intention as my reality. He then proceeded to identify these inner conflicts. They ranged from areas of stress in my life having to do with money, to an earlier unpleasant experience, to unconscious ways that I was compensating for not getting the love I wanted, to limiting beliefs. I was amazed at the depth and scope of the issues that were blocking me. I was also fascinated by the incredible accuracy and speed with which Tom identified these patterns.

My first book, *Chicken Soup for the Soul,* was already written and published when I had that session with Tom. But it was only in the months that followed that the sales really started to take off and the book became the first in a series of best sellers. There are of course many other things that influenced this, but the simple procedures that Tom helped me with during that hour made a real difference between staying stuck in old patterns and being able to break free and create what I really wanted for myself.

Since that time, Tom has worked with thousands of people, helping them to clarify their life purpose, awaken their unique talents, and helping them to remove their inner barriers to having the success in their lives that they truly want. Also in the intervening years, he has been pioneering a whole new field called Human Software Engineering™. It's about finding and fixing the "bugs" in our inner human software, and it is truly groundbreaking work.

In his brilliant book, *Pure Awareness—Five Simple Techniques to Experience Your Essential Nature,* Tom has done something quite unique. He has distilled out of his vast experiences the simplest and most useful tools for creating profound and lasting change in your life. Even more importantly, he has identified exactly what to do to shift your old patterns of thoughts and feelings so that they no longer cause you to respond to life out of your old "knee jerk," conditioned responses.

And if that weren't good enough, he has identified the essence of what you need to actually do in order to cultivate a whole new style of functioning that allows you to, as he says, "respond spontaneously to the needs of the moment with the fullness of your being." This is a potent combination and a whole new way of dismantling unwanted habits. *It is unlike any other program for enriching your life that I've ever seen.*

The unique thing about this book is that it is a practical guide that actually shows you how to really removed your inner barriers and conflicts. Lots of people have written about what you need to do to enjoy a better life; Tom actually gives you the tools for removing the things inside of you that keep tripping you up and getting in your way.

Recently I met with Tom and he showed me how to do the CORE Technique. Wow! I've done plenty of emotional release processing over the years, but this was remarkably simple and especially deep and profound. I came out of something that had been nagging at me for weeks, and when it was complete, I felt a pervasive sense of bliss and expansion.

I am truly grateful to Tom for his help in my life and I am delighted that he is bringing out his work in order to share his insights and techniques. I know his desire is very similar to mine—to have a positive impact on the lives of many, many people. I know that through this book and Tom's pioneering work in creating Human Software Engineering, he will accomplish this goal in a profound and powerful way.

Don't just read this book; actually do what it recommends and you will find your life changing in ways that will inevitably lead you to have a quality of life experience that is beyond your wildest dreams.

— Jack Canfield

Appendix: Additional Resources

To help you get the most out of this book, there is a collection wonderful resources waiting for you at **www.VaporizeYourAnxiety.com/resources.html**

In addition to the resources mentioned throughout this book, you'll find the following:

- Email course that will help you to succeed with these techniques
- Audio and Video with Tom Stone and guests
- Vaporize Your Anxiety Newsletter
- Members' Forum

These resources are all free, and we'll be adding new things to this area of the website all the time. We would appreciate your feedback about the book and the website. Please email us with your suggestions, thoughts, and concerns. Just send an email to **feedback@vaporizeyouranxiety.com.**

And of course, we would love to hear your success stories about using these techniques! You can email them to **success@vaporizeyouranxiety.com.**

Other books by Tom Stone

Pure Awareness—Five Simple Techniques for Experiencing Your Essential Nature

Be Smoke Free Now—Breakthrough Techniques for Becoming a Non-smoker Now and for the Rest of Your Life

These books are available on line at Amazon. Or if you'd like, you can visit **www.VaporizeYourAnxiety.com/books.html**, where you can download free sample chapters, read more about the books, and purchase greatly enhanced eBook versions, which are available for instant download.

Forthcoming titles in the *Vaporize Your Problems* series include:

Vaporize Your Depression
Vaporize Your ADD/ADHD
Vaporize Your Allergies
Vaporize Your Anger
Vaporize Your Fears
(and others...)

The Core Dynamics Seminar on Audio CD

This is a set of 9 audio CDs from a two-day, in depth seminar on the *Core Dynamics of Common Problems* given by Tom Stone. If you're interested in learning as much as you can about Core Dynamics, this is the best resource available. You can order the audio CDs at **www.VaporizeYourAnxiety.com/coredynamics.html**

Other Programs

At the Vaporize Your Anxiety site, you can also find out more about the *Extraordinary Series* and *Vaporize Your Problems* programs we offer.
www.VaporizeYourAnxiety.com/programs.html

Some programs that are available now or will be coming soon include:

Vaporize Your Problems™ Series

Vaporize Your Anxiety
Vaporize Your Depression
Vaporize Your Worries
Vaporize Your Fears
Vaporize Your Loneliness
Vaporize Your Heartbreak
Vaporize Your Grief
Vaporize Your Nervousness
Vaporize Your Resentments
Vaporize Your Emptiness
Vaporize Your Bad Habits
Vaporize Your Anger
Vaporize Your Addictions
Vaporize Your ADD/ADHD
Vaporize Your Allergies

The Great Life Programs™

Extraordinary Prosperity
Extraordinary Relationships
Extraordinary Wellness

For a complete list of Books, Audio and Video Recordings, Products, and Programs by Tom Stone, please visit:
www.VaporizeYourAnxiety.com/catalog.html

Core Dynamics Coaching

I've mentioned Core Dynamics Coaching several times throughout this book. I'd like to go into a little more depth here. Life Coaching has become one of the biggest sectors of the helping professions in the U.S., and it is growing dramatically in Europe, Asia and Australia as well. I have spoken at coaching seminars all over the world, and I am thrilled to witness the growing interest in this approach to helping people resolve their problems and get more of what they want from life.

Core Dynamics Coaching is very different than traditional life coaching, however. Our founding principle is that only great people can be truly great coaches. Core Dynamics Coaches go through a rigorous 6-month program that includes extensive training in the CORE Technique, allowing them to vaporize their own deepest emotional pain, fears, traumas and demons. This liberates their natural greatness and allows their Highest Self to shine through. They become experts on all the *Pure Awareness Techniques* discussed in this book, and they receive training on many advanced techniques not covered here. They come out the other side of the training program as transformed individuals and highly effective coaches.

Core Dynamics Coach Training is not appropriate for everyone, and we only accept people who exhibit a strong potential for creating a powerful, clean coaching presence. To become certified, each candidate must have in-depth knowledge of each of the Core Dynamics, must have a comprehensive understanding of the nature of pre-verbal conditioning, and must be highly proficient using both the Core Dynamics Coaching protocol and the Pure Awareness Techniques.

Great Life Technologies has already certified many Core Dynamics Coaches who are now helping their clients vaporize anxiety and other problems that have been plaguing them their entire lives.

The clients of Core Dynamics coaches tend to experience rapid and profound breakthroughs that conventional coaches can't achieve because they don't have access to the necessary techniques.

If you've had any coaching in the past, you owe it to yourself to experience Core Dynamics Coaching firsthand. You'll be amazed at how powerful and different it is.

When you visit **www.VaporizeYourAnxiety.com/coaches.html**, you will find a directory of Core Dynamics Coaches. You'll be able to browse the faculty of Master Coaches, and find one that seems like the right fit for you.

Core Dynamics Coach Training

You would not be alone if you found that your exposure to the techniques in this book sparked an interest in becoming a certified Core Dynamics Coach yourself! In fact, many of our Master Coaches began as clients of mine. They were people with no background in coaching at all. But once they began to experience dramatic breakthroughs in their own lives, they suddenly realized they had developed a strong desire to share the power of Core Dynamics Coaching with others.

The Core Dynamics Coach Training course, which is generally taught twice per year, teaches all the techniques for becoming a Certified Core Dynamics Coach. It also prepares students for International Coach Federation (ICF) Certification through a unique approach to the eleven Core Competencies that are the foundation of the

ICF Credentialing process. The program begins with a four-day live seminar taught by myself and Michael Stratford, the co-founder of Core Dynamics Coaching.

The training then continues over four and a half months with live online classes and personal coaching sessions

You can get all the information about Core Dynamics Coach Training at: **www.VaporizeYourAnxiety.com/coachtraining.html**

This text was set in Magma, an elegant sans serif typeface designed by Tom's brother, Sumner Stone, of the Stone Type Foundry.

www.stonetypefoundry.com

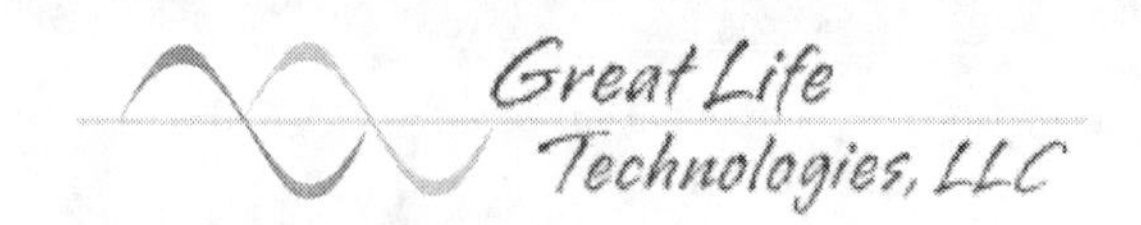

Quick Book Order Form

Online orders:	www.VaporizeYourAnxiety.com/books.html
Email orders:	orders@www.VaporizeYourAnxiety.com
Telephone orders:	(619) 557-2700
Fax orders:	(619) 557-8446
Postal orders:	Great Life Technologies, 7040 Avenida Encinas, Suite 104 #380, Carlsbad, CA 92011

Please send the following books ($20.00 each):

☐ **Be Smoke-Free Now** QTY: ____________

☐ **Pure Awareness** QTY: ____________

☐ **Vaporize Your Anxiety** QTY: ____________

Subtotal: ____________

*California residents add 7.25% Sales Tax: ____________

Shipping: $5.00 for first book, $2.00 for each additional book. International: $10.00 for first book, $2.00 for each additional item. ____________

TOTAL: ____________

Please include information about:

☐ Core Dynamics Coaching

☐ Core Dynamics Newsletter

☐ Tom Stone's Speaking Engagements

Billing Address:

Name: ____________

Address: ____________

City: ________ State: ____ Zip: ____

Email: ____________

Telephone: ____________

Shipping Address (if different):

Name: ____________

Address: ____________

City: ________ State: ____ Zip: ____

Email: ____________

Telephone: ____________

Payment:

Check ☐ Credit Card: ☐ Visa ☐ M/C ☐ Amex

Name as it appears on card: ____________

Card number: ____________

Expiration Date: ________ / ________